THE CANTOS
OF EZRA POUND

Also by Eugene Paul Nassar

Wallace Stevens: An Anatomy of Figuration
The Rape of Cinderella: Essays in Literary Continuity

Eugene Paul Nassar

THE CANTOS
OF EZRA POUND
The Lyric Mode

THE JOHNS HOPKINS UNIVERSITY PRESS
Baltimore and London

The Johns Hopkins University Press, Baltimore, Maryland 21218
The Johns Hopkins Press Ltd., London

Library of Congress Catalog Card Number 75-11343
ISBN 0-8018-1703-X

Originally published, 1975
Second printing, 1976

Library of Congress Cataloging in Publication data
will be found on the last printed page of this book.

To
Karen, my wife,
to
Anne and Laura,
and to the welcome children
that may come

# CONTENTS

 PREFACE

I have tried to provide in this study what it
seemed to me the serious student of Pound
and *The Cantos* needed in the present state of the studies of Ezra
Pound: a coherent overview and a detailed analysis of the lyrical
passages in *The Cantos*. "Lyrical" is used in the broad sense, to
encompass passages in Pound that dramatize aesthetic or psychic
experience, using the language of symbol and myth, accompanied
often, though not always, by an elevation of diction and melody.
It is clearly demonstrable that these passages have a continuity that,
demonstrated, may help the student toward a more precise sense
of the overall continuities of thought, attitude, and technique in
The Cantos. The basic position of this book is that the central or
root attitudes of the poem, what might properly be called its
tonality, are "dualistic," as I try to define the word throughout

the text. This is not to say that Pound does not have a theological position, only that Pound is earth-oriented. Nor is he the "broken bundle of mirrors," the craftsman incapable of sustained thought, theological or otherwise, that hostile criticism or metacriticism would make him. Pound is himself, as he sees Ovid, "urbane, skeptical" (*vide The Spirit of Romance,* p. 15), but he can also say, "I consider the writings of Confucius and Ovid's *Metamorphoses* the only safe guides in religion" (*Letters,* p. 183). In my analyses of the aesthetic functioning of the gods and goddesses which populate the lyric passages of *The Cantos,* I may, at times, and for some readers of Pound, shave a verity in Pound's mental world. But to do so is preferable to me than to talk of the cosmic consciousness or of conscious or unconscious archetypes, which does not explain details of a text or convince those not already true believers.

The reader will, I hope, excuse a certain amount of repetition in the analyses. I cannot expect most readers to read each chapter but, rather, to consult those pages which handle a passage or motif in which the reader is interested. I have translated foreign phrases where I feel translation is necessary, especially in the post-*Pisan Cantos,* where the student is as yet without the aid of an *Annotated Index* type of glossary. My references to *The Cantos* follow the system developed by Professor Hugh Kenner in *The Pound Era:* the first reference (if necessary) is to the canto number (in arabic numbers); page numbers within cantos refer, first, to the 1970 New Directions collected edition (offset from earlier editions) of Cantos 1–117, and, second, to the 1964 Faber edition of Cantos 1–109. Faber citations for Cantos 110–17 are from the 1970 *Drafts and Fragments of Cantos CX–CXVII.* Page references to other works of Pound are from the New Directions editions and to works by others from the editions cited in the Bibliography.

My interest in Pound was sparked more than a decade ago by Professor Arthur Mizener, and I have been at *The Cantos* since then, using the resources of the fine Pound collection at Hamilton College, Clinton, New York. My thanks go to Walter

Pilkington, Director, Helene Browning, Betty Wallace, and Frank Lorenz for their kind assistance at the library. Pat Dugan and Sylvia Rathbun at the Utica College Library were untiring in their efforts on my behalf. I have had the benefit of the scholarship of the late Rocco LoPardo, who studied Greek, Latin, French, Italian, and Provençal with the same teachers, though later, that Pound had had at Hamilton College. Mr. LoPardo's knowledge of the languages was matched by his insight into Pound's intentions in his quotations from these languages. John Moses, of the same school, also gave me valuable help in the classical languages. William P. Sisler and Olga Kessel of the Johns Hopkins University Press have guided my manuscript through the publication process with thoughtfulness and skill. My thanks go also to Merna Schaub, especially, and to Grace Dempsey, Katherine Ellis, and Martha Hanson for typing the various drafts of the manuscript.

Several paragraphs of chapter 2 have been taken from my article "Illusion as Value: An Essay on a Modern Poetic Idea," which appeared in *Mosaic:* A Journal for the Comparative Study of Literature and Ideas, published by the University of Manitoba Press, vol. 7, no. 4 (July 1974), and a short section of chapter 5 originally appeared as "This Stone Giveth Sleep': 'Io Son la Luna" in *Paideuma,* vol. 1, no. 2 (Winter 1972); both are reprinted by permission of the journals.

I received kind and helpful answers to inquiries of mine from Professors Walter Baumann, Guy Davenport, Donald Gallup, Eva Hesse, and Hugh Kenner, and from Princess Mary DeRachewiltz, Pound's daughter. My debt to previous Pound scholars and critics will be obvious in the text and notes. Much Poundian scholarship now, necessarily, deals with Pound's sources. It is the critic's job, then, to study *The Cantos*, in Hugh Kenner's words, "not where the components come from, but how they go together" (*The Poetry of Ezra Pound,* 1951, p. 14). This book, while doing perhaps its small share of source identification, attempts to make more precise just how and why the images "go together" in Pound's lyric mode.

THE CANTOS
OF EZRA POUND

 1: INTRODUCTION

Variously called Pound's "lyrical moments,"
"visionary experience," or the
"mythological element," certain passages throughout *The
Cantos* have always been appreciated by the poet's readers,
especially those who are, for various reasons, hostile to the work
as a whole. It is my feeling that critical precision concerning *The
Cantos* as a whole can come only from some greater precision of
analysis of those key passages where the poet's power is most
generally felt. Serious criticism of *The Cantos* has, it seems to
me, been established at quite a high level (disregarding the
popular journals) since the appearance of *The Pisan Cantos* but
has avoided, in the main, close analysis of the visionary passages
in question, as if such analysis might, as it were, break the spell.
The passages have been handled, when at all, via constant

3

reference to Pound's prose, to his sources, and to the more discursive sections of *The Cantos.* Criticism certainly ought to operate from the opposite direction; the primary interpretive data ought to be the radiant lyric nodes of *The Cantos* themselves; secondary, and in descending order, ought to be the nonlyrical portions of *The Cantos,* Pound's other poetry, his prose, and, finally, his sources. The tonality—the actually achieved and complex body of attitudes at the center of Pound's creative imagination in this immense work—is most precisely focused there, where it is most deeply felt and most successfully communicated. And I submit that that tonality, accurately grasped, causes certain "bewildering" effects in Pound to become clear and, in the process, certain problems and issues constantly in critical debate seem to disappear or to become side issues.

Much of the Pound literature (as of all critical literature) consists of metacritical squabbles over Pound's attitudes toward history, politics, philosophy, religion, and art, and much of the heat is generated (as always) by critic X's prohibition of the application to Pound of categorical terms like *nominalist* or *Platonist, symbolist* or *dualist,* when it is perfectly clear to critic Y that all or some of these terms must apply. The terms apply, of course, as their definitions apply; critic Z would work, as I advocate, from the lyric texts outward and define his terms to fit the contexts.

Dualist—by my definition—Pound certainly is, to the very core of his art. It is indeed the burden of this essay that Pound's deepest intuitions as expressed in the lyrical passages continually affirm man's made beauty ("crystal" from "water") in the face of inevitable cyclic drift toward dissolution, personal and societal. But it is not a Manichean dualism; there is no worship of and no exultation in the darkness, in the conflict of Yin and Yang; there is only acceptance. Likewise with nominalist. Used strictly, as with certain medieval scholastics, to mean that Platonic absolutes, ideals, forms, or universals do not exist (as

opposed to the realist's doctrine that the universals are "real"),
Pound would repudiate any such denying of felt (though
ineffable) energies in the universe. Yet, nominalist Pound is—
nominalist used expansively, in the sense that, while words in
poetic texts do have a magical effect on one's mood, words and
metaphors encompass no absolute or transcendental truth. As
with nominalist, so with Platonist.[1] Finally, Pound abhors the
word *symbol,* as it might refer to a concept of fixed counters of
representation interchangeable from one literary context to
another. He prefers the term *image* to represent a complex of
figures in a unique context. "Archetypal" symbols are as
repugnant to Pound as dogma in religion. But, as I hope to
demonstrate, Pound *is* a symbolist, allegorist, emblemist in his
lyric modes, the figurative language creating its unique context
("vortex," "node," "cluster") of mood and meaning locally,
and, by iteration, in the whole poem. Symbolism, in this sense,
is as vital to Pound as is ritual in religion.[2]

One reaches for precision of these abstract terms not for
ultimate, absolute definitions, but for the sense of them in one
poet like Pound—in his context, his continuum. The thumbnail
sketch, above, of some of his major attitudes depends on
whether or not it is a true a posteriori summation of *The
Cantos'* central dynamics—that is, on the precision and accuracy
of the analyses below. The early poetry of Pound and his prose
statements often do corroborate what one feels a passage of *The
Cantos* is about, but the analysis below uses these only to
supplement, not to establish, what the canto passage itself ought
to communicate. Hugh Witemeyer, in fact, in his excellent *The
Poetry of Ezra Pound 1908-1920* (especially in the chapter
entitled "Delightful Psychic Experience") brings together much
of the relevant materials besides those in *The Cantos* and
summarizes Pound's major attitudes much as I have summarized
them. Witemeyer, for instance, demonstrates Pound's care to
distinguish myth from transcendent reality in his prose. "Myths,"
Pound says, "are explications of mood," "equations for the

human emotions"; the artist makes myth an "impersonal or objective story woven out of his own emotion." It is the complex tonalities of these emotions, as they establish themselves through the effects of a precisely controlled language in the mythic or lyrical or visionary passages, and the continuity of these emotions, that I hope to trace through *The Cantos*— that is, to try to do the job Clark Emery calls for with respect to the "mythological pattern" in such passages. He states that "To determine the status of Pound's soul at any given point in these Cantos requires the most precise possible definition of the mythic images and a clear understanding of the function of the lyric high points" (*Ideas into Action,* p.129). Noel Stock, in his *Reading the Cantos,* speaks of the "mythological puzzle, which, solved, will aid us towards the meaning" (p. 57). Apologies for butchering, through analysis, a lyric passage in *The Cantos* are standard procedure in Pound literature,[3] but this is not to say that analysis must be butchery, that it cannot move toward some illuminating precision.

First, to summarize findings. It has been my experience in studying *The Cantos* in the past few years that the contextual implications (philosophic, religious, aesthetic) of the lyric or visionary or mythological passages of the earlier cantos flow beautifully into the deeper and wider implications of those of the later cantos, that not only the mood or tonality of mind in these lyric passages is continuous but also the mode. The imagery and diction in these passages creates a special language that keeps developing and flowering in such a way as to make the visions of the late cantos (say, 90–117) a true culmination aesthetically (I would say also philosophically) of the whole. The later lyric passages are a true efflorescence of the earlier— the potential of the lyric seedbed realized, Pound's particular crystal vision achieved. I will only remark in passing on the nonlyric passages in *The Cantos,* but it will be clear that I find them, in general, a fitting counterfoil to the lyric passages. So that while the limits of this essay restrict discussion of the unity of the whole poem, it presumes to help make more precise such discussion in the future.

The chapters to follow settle down necessarily into a chronological explication; a précis of what I find to be the major epistemological attitudes that impel Pound's lyrics, and some of the figurations used to represent these attitudes, is in order. The page references cite a few occurrences of what often may be a leitmotif running throughout *The Cantos*.

The central image of the crystal[4] represents for Pound, as I have implied above, an achieved aesthetic act of completeness and magnitude, one coherent context among other gems. The aesthetic act, of which no one can know the transcendental relation, is performed in the mind of the artist, represented as a "maze" (793:23), a "labyrinth" (799:29), a "mirror" (66, 8: 70, 2) or a "hall of mirrors" (793:23), through the faculty of intuition or imagination, represented by the figures of the "flame" (27:31, 196:204), the "torch" (78:82, 236:246), and "light" (passim). The creative flame "builds light" (642:675), has throughout *The Cantos* its "moments" (11:15; the "blue flash," 802:32) of "delightful psychic experience," whence it "makes" gods and goddesses (195:203). These subjective visions are rooted in objective perceptions ("mint, thyme, basilicum," 435:463) and colored by these ("Topaz I manage and three shades of blue," 17:21; "The wind is dyed in your valley," 689:719). One's mind, and hence one's art, is limited to one's place ("Art is local," 678:708), one's context ("My Sordello?" 6:10; "Whose world, or mine, or theirs?" 521:556). Whatever gods there may be, our subjective, creative eye is "God in us" (685:715; "God's eye art thou," 790:20). Dante's vision of a god of pure light is denied us (the "Nous" is "ineffable," 201:209); Pound's goddesses populating *The Cantos* (and the earlier poetry) have always "cloaks," "scarves," "sheaths," "gauzes," about them, representing the limiting "diaphans" (177:182, 644:677) or clouds of perception. These limits are variously represented as the "half-light" (13:17, 17:21), as

"hypostasis" (520:551), and as the "mind's space" (786:16).
Also as a "cave" (76:80, 238:248) beneath or within a
"mountain" or "hill" (passim) where we enter via "stairs,"
"gates," or "doors" of perception or vision[5] to receive what we
can of blessedness (our "paradise terrestre" 802:32), and out of
which crystal water (15:19, "Castalia," 605:639) flows. The
spiritual adventurer or "sailor" (Odysseus or other) in his travels
by "boat" (77-79:81-83) or "raft" (92-94:96-98) enters at
times the mind's place (the "new air," 69:73, 238:248, "ver
novum," 195:204, 570:606), "that place" (90:94, 458:486) of
flowering "almond trees,"[6] representing the lyric state of mind.
The mind's art transforms cold stone into marble goddesses[7] and
marble cities, creates visions that are free-floating[8] (cf. "leaf
without root," "grape without seed," 7:11) because they are
not real until the mind achieves them. Thus the artist's
achievement is "not of the sun" (76:80) but of one's crystal
vision, and lasting, radiant, only until inevitable "seepage"
(576:612, 789:19) occurs. Destructive reality, wind, wave,
"sea-claw" and "sea-wrack,"[9] is always being transformed, out
of "erebus" (3:7), "out of nothing" (8:12), by the creative
spirit into gentle animals (Canto 2 and passim) or zephyrs
(238:248, 435:461) or gems to an aesthetic (spiritual?) stillness
(245:256) out of the noise of eternal wave motion.

But Pound will never deny the reality of sea-wrack, of the
tragic dualism that is embodied in *The Cantos* to the smallest
details. Confucius cannot "keep the blossoms from falling"
(60:64); mud and light, gold and gloom, good and evil (Ra-set in
her barge, 684:714) is the law of life ("rain also is of the
process," 425:451), and the lyric Pound is not at any moment
avoiding the fact; the language is of the two, in the constant
figuration of "little light in a great darkness" (795:25), and of
"narrow paths" (66:70, 746:771, cf. "gold thread," 797:27,
"hair's breadth," 632:664) to the one shrine or temple, the
"heart's field" (792:22). All of which leads one to the great

lyric of Canto 81, the emotional, philosophical, and aesthetic
center of the whole.

> Saw but the eyes and stance between the eyes
> colour, diastasis,
> careless or unaware it had not the
> whole tent's room
> nor was place for the full Ειδώς [Knowing] . . .

> What thou lovest well remains,
> the rest is dross
> What thou lov'st well shall not be reft from thee
> What thou lov'st well is thy true heritage
> Whose world, or mine or theirs
> or is it of none?

[81/520:556]

The vision (of "Aphrodite's" eyes) is limited but loved;
subjective, perhaps unreal objectively, but loved. It is the most
beautiful yet baldest statement of an epistemology bathed in
dualism, which controls the movement and imagery of the
whole poem.

The later cantos, which are still suffering under the spell of
The Pisan Cantos, superbly inweave the lyric imagery of the
cantos preceding, but because they do so with an earned
ellipticity, they do not easily render themselves up to the reader
who has not sensed the patterns of imagery in the earlier cantos.
The later cantos, for example, are full of references to *muan
bpo* (Cantos 101, 102, 104, 110, 112), an ancient ritual of
China, which can look to the skeptical eye as a primitive and
pointless late excursion for a mind of Pound's sophistication.
But it is precisely the crystalline purity of a mind caught up in
beauty, a loved context of ritual and belief, that captures the
heart of the sophisticated Pound. It is but the last representation
of Pound's joy in the aesthetic wholeness and wholesomeness of
man and society within ritual, from Eleusis to *Li Ki,* medieval
cathedral building, the Sienese religious festival of Canto 43, the

priest's first mass of Canto 48. Pound is a devotee of no specific ritual or belief, but is respectful of and pleased by those which he feels lend light and order to life, so heavily compounded of darkness and disorder.

 2: CANTOS 1-16

In 1925 there appeared *A Draft of XVI Cantos,* in a limited edition (90 copies). In June, July, and August 1917 *Poetry Magazine* had published "Three Cantos," parts of which were salvaged and rearranged for the 1925 volume. Most of what is now Canto 2 appeared first in *Dial* magazine in May 1922 as "Eighth Canto" and found its present position in the 1925 volume. These sixteen cantos, as they come first, have been subject to much explication, especially in the *Analyst* sheets from Northwestern University. I shall only examine the lyrical passages in these early cantos in order to establish their tonality within a dualistic framework, a tonality that I hope to show is the keynote or ground bass of *The Cantos,* early or late.

          Sweet lie!—Was I there truly? . . .
             Let's believe it. . . .
                    No, take it all for lies
I have but smelt this life, a whiff of it—
               . . . And shall I claim;
Confuse my own phantastikon,
Or say the filmy shell that circumscribes me
Contains the actual sun;
                  confuse the thing I see
With actual gods behind me?
                 Are they gods behind me?
How many worlds we have! If Botticelli
Brings her ashore on that great cockle-shell—
His Venus (Simonetta?),
And Spring and Aufidus fill all the air
With their clear-outlined blossoms?
World enough. Behold, I say, she comes
"Apparelled like the spring, Graces her subjects,"
(That's from *Pericles*).
Oh, we have worlds enough, and brave *décors,*
And from these like we guess a soul for man
And build him full of aery populations.
            [*Poetry*, "Canto I," June 1917, pp. 120–21]

No part of this passage survived in the 1925 edition. "Canto I" in *Poetry*, clearly a preliminary working out of Pound's intentions for a long poem, is an interior monologue addressed to Robert Browning. The passage is not lyric in mode, but an apologia for the lyric mood. The mind circumscribed by its diaphanous film—its limits—imagines gods when in the presence of beauty (Botticelli's Venus, or other "brave *décors*"). The mind as "phantastikon" may be intuiting transcendent truths or it may be lying to itself, but no matter. Lie or no, the mind's psychic experience in the presence of beauty is "World enough."

    The language of the passage is so clearly and carefully accommodating a mood of self-irony that if it had remained in *The Cantos* the image of a neo-Platonistic, mystic-leaning Pound would not be as fashionable as it is. This is also the case

in a lengthy passage in *Poetry*'s "Canto III" and its redaction in
Lustra, 1918, where Pound muses on various neo-Platonists,
figures to which he returns later in *The Cantos*. The detached,
rather superior handling of Proclus, Psellus, Porphyry, Ficino,
Valla, and finally John Heydon ("a half-cracked fellow . . . seer
of pretty visions . . . full of a plaintive charm . . . Munching
Ficino's mumbling Platonists"), makes it clear that Pound is not
a devotee.

Pound again is clear and direct (and perhaps less effective
than in the later elliptical manner) in the early *Poetry* versions in
comparing his aesthetic and philosophic problems with those of
Robert Browning, author of *Sordello*.

> . . . what were the use
> Of setting figures up and breathing life upon them,
> Were't not *our* life, your life, my life extended?
> I walk Verona. (I am here in England.)
> I see Can Grande. (Can see whom you will.)
>   You had one whole man?
> And I have many fragments, less worth? Less worth?
> Ah, had you quite my age, quite such a beastly and
>   cantankerous age?
> You had some basis, had some set belief.
>   [*Poetry*, "Canto I," June 1917, p. 115]

The only modern form that can capture one's beastly age in the
absence of a set belief is, Pound feels, the "rag bag" or "fish-net"
(p. 113). He asks of such a form, "has it a place in music?" (p.
115). All of this confessional tentativeness and directly expressed
unsureness is stripped from the final versions of the opening
cantos, though the absolute fidelity to the chaos of the modern
world and experience remains, that is, the "fish-net" form.

Stripped are such revealing lines of sophisticated self-irony
as "Whom shall I hang my shimmering garment on; / Who wear
my feathery mantle, *hagoromo*; / Whom set to dazzle the serious
future ages?" (p. 117). If one reads the Noh play *Hagoromo*
(which Pound had earlier translated from the Japanese), one

senses the serious commitment of the poet to the magic of the aesthetic moment; the last line of the *Poetry* passage blends with the tone of seriousness the tone of self-mockery of a poem like the *Homage to Sextus Propertius* (which Pound dates at 1917 in *Personae*), a poem skeptical of the gods and much else. The tonality rendered is complex, combining the attitudes of a "priest" of art and that of a skeptic, a tonality cultivated by Pound during the period 1913–19, and one that is natural to a temperament not sure whether one's gods are phantasy but quite sure that one will not give up one's gods. Such a voice or mask runs through the *Lustra* and *Propertius* poems and is clearly a conscious attempt by the poet to encompass a tonal range wider than that of the worshipful attitude toward beauty and art while still including this attitude.

The poems in *Personae* dated through 1912 are full of the priest-artist worshiping his lady (Beauty, Vision). There is no better poem of this mode than "A Virginal."

> No, no! Go from me. I have left her lately.
> I will not spoil my sheath with lesser brightness,
> For my surrounding air hath a new lightness;
> Slight are her arms, yet they have bound me straitly
> And left me cloaked as with a gauze of aether;
> As with sweet leaves; as with subtle clearness.
> Oh, I have picked up magic in her nearness
> To sheathe me half in half the things that sheathe her.
> No, no! Go from me. I have still the flavour.
> Soft as spring wind that's come from birchen bowers.
> Green come the shoots, aye April in the branches,
> As winter's wound with her sleight hand she staunches,
> Hath of the trees a likeness of the savour;
> As white their bark, so white this lady's hours.

The woman told to go is any real woman, who cannot inspire the exultation of mood the mind enwrapped in beauty can summon. The "sheath," "cloak," and "gauze" are all variations recurring throughout the early *Personae* poems to represent the ability of the artist's creative yet limited mind to make the universe lovely in its "hours," the psychic moment figured by the radiant white light. "Erat Hora" gives thanks for the one sunlit hour of the "Lady's" appearance or manifestation. Such an apparition is implied in the title of the poem "Apparuit," where the figuration is of dawn light flowing over a marvelous "House" (a variation on the stock "Palace of Art" motif), and especially over an alabaster statue of a goddess in a portal of the house. The carven "fabric" and the sun's golden "weft" are components of the goddess's "sheath." The poet's mind laments the loss of its "sheath," its moment or "hour," but the transience of the aesthetic moment is as inevitable as dawn's passing. "The House of Splendor" is but a more transparent allegory of the artist's mind's worship of its own "moments" ("My Lady") and those of others ("There are many rooms") in the dwelling of Beauty.

"The Alchemist," dated 1912, unpublished till 1920, is a transitional poem that begins to develop the more complex attitudes toward art and beauty that culminate in *The Cantos.* The Lady figure in this poem is fragmented to a chant of names of ladies that have inspired lyric poets, in a prayer that art do for the modern poet what it has done for poets of earlier ages, the transmuting of base metal (reality) into the gold of the imagination.

> O Queen of Cypress,
> Out of Erebus, the flat-lying breadth,
> Breath that is stretched out beneath the world:
> Out of Erebus, out of the flat waste of air, lying
>   beneath the world;
> Out of the brown leaf-brown colourless
>   Bring the imperceptible cool.

Air without the spirit's myths is hell, or "Erebus"; color and cool relief come from dreams, meditations, the "magic" rituals and chants of poetry. The poem, with its large measure of sophistication and ironic distance, was not included in the 1912 *Ripostes* volume, but only in *Umbra,* in 1920, when the experiments of the *Lustra* poems and the *Homage to Sextus*

Propertius developed fully the tone of worship/non-worship of art and beauty, of the Lady. The 1917 cantos in *Poetry Magazine* show the poet in the process of deciding that the big poem he had been contemplating for years would have to be, to be true to perception, a "rag bag," to be of both Erebus and the Lady.

Erebus and the Lady are the matter, certainly, of Canto 1 as we now have it. Homer's land of the shades, as projected through Pound, is a fair version of the human condition in its cycles of suffering, endurance, and tragedy. The Aphrodite passage at the end of the canto is a fair version of recurrent ecstatic moments in human experience. The gods that may be behind the veils of nature, and the rites to the gods, give configurations of meaning to the sailors' lives (be they Odysseus or the Anglo-Saxon seafarer). Pound intends Canto 1 as a paradigm of the human condition and a paradigm of all that is to come in the whole poem. So that he can well end the canto (as he did not end it in the *Poetry* version, where it appears, not first, but merely as the ending to "Canto III") with "So that." The earliest poetry in Western literature had already provided the paradigm of the human condition, its tragedy and triumphs; what can later poets—Sordello of the thirteenth century, Browning in the nineteenth century, or Pound in the twentieth— do but weave subjective variations on the same permanent themes of Erebus and the Lady?

Almost all of *Poetry*'s "Canto I"—so discursive, confessional, and tentative—is stricken; what is kept is reduced in Canto 2 as we now have it to "Hang it all, Robert Browning, / There can be but the one Sordello. / But Sordello, and my Sordello?" Three poets—the actual Sordello ("Lo Sordels si fo di Montovana") and both Browning and Pound writing about him—are all really expressing themselves, their personal visions of moments of heaven and of hell. So, too, a bit later in the canto, does So-shu, Oriental writer, voyager, "using the long

moon for a churn-stick." That is, all artists of all times look at
life's processes (wave motion) and transform objective fact
(lovely or otherwise) into a subjective reality.

> Seal sports in the spray-whited circles of cliff-wash,
> Sleek head, daughter of Lir,
>   eyes of Picasso
> Under black fur-hood, lithe daughter of Ocean

To see Lir's (or Oceanus') daughter's head, or Picasso's eyes, in
the sporting seal is a purely subjective transformation, having
nothing to do with a transcendental insight. Likewise with the
following:

> And the wave runs in the beach-groove:
> Eleanor, . . .

> And by the beach-run, Tyro
>   Twisted arms of the sea-god,
> Lithe sinews of water, gripping her, cross-hold,
> And the blue-gray glass of the wave tents them,
> Glare azure of water, cold-welter, close cover . . .

> And by Scios,
>   to left of the Naxos passage,
> Naviform rock overgrown,
>   algae cling to its edge,
> There is a wine-red glow in the shallows,
>   a tin flash in the sun-dazzle.

Three events of the imagination are elliptically linked here by
the conjunction *and* (as are all events in the canto and, often, in
the whole poem). Poets (Pound is saying) listen to the waves,
look at the cold gray color of the ocean, and populate its flux
with personages—of, say, old men murmuring of Helens of Troy
(Homer's "ear" for the sea-surge) or Eleanors of Acquitaine;
wave rolling on wave can be seen as an embrace of a Neptune
and Tyro; a wine-red glow in the shallows can conjure up the
legend of the wine god, Bacchus.

And by the rock-pool a young boy loggy with vine-must, . . .

God-sleight then, god-sleight . . .
Beasts like shadows in glass,
   a furred tail upon nothingness . . .
void air taking pelt.
Lifeless air become sinewed, . . .
   And I worship.
I have seen what I have seen.

The voice is that of a sailor who watched Bacchus turn empty
ocean and air into a menagerie. Pound takes the myth from
Ovid's *Metamorphoses* and makes it new, makes it his own as
one example ("and . . . and") of the poetic imagination's
eternally metamorphosing natural process into personal or
public myth.

And of a later year,
   pale in the wine-red algae,
If you will lean over the rock,
   the coral face under wave-tinge,
Rose-paleness under water-shift,
    Ileuthyeria, fair Dafne of sea-bords,
The swimmer's arms turned to branches,
Who will say in what year,
   fleeing what band of tritons,
The smooth brows, seen, and half seen,
   now ivory stillness.
And So-shu churned in the sea, So-shu also,
   using the long moon for a churn-stick . . .
Lithe turning of water,
   sinews of Poseidon,
Black azure and hyaline,
   glass wave over Tyro,
Close cover, unstillness,
   bright welter of wave-cords . . .

And we have heard the fauns chiding Proteus
   in the smell of hay under the olive-trees,
And the frogs singing against the fauns
   in the half-light.
And . . .

The "you" addressed is the sensitive reader, the "you" becomes the more intimate "we" as the reader is initiated into the worship of the poetic consciousness of any time or nation ("So-shu also") that transforms in the mind wave-tinge to rose Ileuthyeria, wave motion to fleeing tritons, hay smell and half-light into fauns. The conjunctions, the linkages of examples can be endless (Protean), for the imagination's deifying process is endless.

The poetic consciousness is ever transforming "void," "lifeless" air (cf. the "flat waste of air," or "erebus," of "The Alchemist") into "sheaths" (cf. the Lady's "sheaths" in "A Virginal"). Images of powerful, yet domesticated animals, "leopards," "panthers," and "lynxes," represent in the following passage the power of the creative imagination:

> And, out of nothing, a breathing . . .
>   . . . a furred tail upon nothingness.
> Lynx-purr, and heathery smell of beasts,
>   where tar smell had been,
> Sniff and pad-foot of beasts,
>   eye-glitter out of black air . . .
> Rustle of airy sheaths,
>   dry forms in the *aether* . . .
>   void air taking pelt.
> Lifeless air become sinewed,
>   feline leisure of panthers,
> Leopards . . .

To smell heather where tar smell had been, and from leopards and panthers, is a conscious absurdity to enforce Pound's theme that the moment of "vision" is both "divine" and irrational. Leopards and panthers are used for the same effect in the poem "Heather" in *Personae,* and these central images and others (such as the lynx) in Canto 2 recur often in *The Cantos* (cf. "ac ferae familiares," 94:98; 457:486).

Canto 2, in fact, seems to me to be Pound's most crucial achievement until *The Pisan Cantos.* It was written in 1922, after Pound had been at *The Cantos* for at least five years, published in the *Dial* as the "Eighth Canto," and given its place

of prominence in the 1925 volume. It seems to me central to all
of his thought and style in *The Cantos* from then on, the
dominant vortex piece (together, perhaps, with Canto 17) to
which he continually returns. The poet, after developing many
variations (linked by the "and . . . and" motif) on poetic modes
of seeing, asks,

> Who will say in what year
> > fleeing what band of tritons,
> The smooth brows, seen, and half seen,
> > now ivory stillness.

He is thus describing what early becomes the major
epistemological position of *The Cantos,* as expressed in the great
"libretto" or lyric of Canto 81. The image of Aphrodite's eyes
("brows . . . half seen"), or the image of Bacchus out of the
wine-red color of light on wave, is the image of partial vision, of
"half-light" (cf. "hypostasis," "half-mask's space," in Canto
81/520:555). The "unstillness, bright welter of wave cords" is
transformed in the mind's aesthetic moments and achievements
to the "ivory stillness" (cf. the "palpable Elysium" of Canto
81/521:556), though the moments for the artist will come and
go, as wave or wind. The wave image dominates Canto 2, the
wind image to the same purpose dominates *The Pisan Cantos,*
and culminates in Canto 81 in the lines:

> Ed ascoltando al leggier mormorio
> > [and listening to the light murmur of the wind]
> > there came new subtlety of eyes into my tent,
> whether of spirit or hypostasis . . .

> > > > > > > > > [81/520:555]

Pound listens to the wind as Homer listened to the waves in
Canto 2, and has his personal truth come to him. And it does
not matter if it be a transcendent or subjective truth: "Whose
world, or mine or theirs / or is it of none?" [81/521:556].
Despite the possibility that "the drama is wholly subjective"
(p. 430:457), the poet can never cease transforming through

loving, for without desire there is no life.

Canto 3, like Canto 1, counterpoises moments of lyrical stillness with moments of action in the world of particulars. El Cid is but one variation on the Ulysses figure, one who lived a life in one way or another worth living, one who creates a context, or some sort of society, worth having or knowing. These men, like Sigismundo, Adams, Jefferson, Federico, Confucius, Hanno, and others, and their contrasting figures, those who have not created a worthwhile context, or who have created a bad context, are not within the scope of this essay, though the bulk of *The Cantos* is concerned with discriminations between such figures and their contexts. The dynamism of Pound's heroes and their achievements is always seen in the larger context of "unstillness," of walls stripped of frescoes, of tapestries in tatters. The tragic tone of this larger context gives precise meaning to all of the discursive, narrative sections of *The Cantos,* and this dualistic tonality is most intensely and completely expressed in the lyric passages.

> Gods float in the azure air,
> Bright gods and Tuscan, back before dew was shed.
> Light: and the first light, before ever dew was fallen.
> Panisks, and from the oak, dryas,
> And from the apple, maelid,
> Through all the wood, and the leaves are full of voices,
> A-whisper, and the clouds bowe over the lake,
> And there are gods upon them.
>
> [3/11:15]

To feel the immediate presence of gods in the trees about you is an experience almost lost to the modern mind; it belongs to the "first light, before ever dew was fallen," that is, before religious man learned to distrust his visionary imagination. The problem Pound externalizes here is one of circularity: Imagination needs belief and belief needs imagination. The problem had been meditated upon more discursively in the original "Canto I" in *Poetry,* in which this lyric passage occurs in its earliest form.

> Gods float in the azure air,
> Bright gods, and Tuscan, back before dew was shed,
> It is a world like Puvis'?
>   Never so pale, my friend,
> 'Tis the first light—not half light—Panisks
> And oak-girls and the Maenads
> Have all the wood. Our olive Sirmio
> Lies in its burnished mirror, and the Mounts Balde and Riva
> Are alive with song, and all the leaves are full of voices.
> *"Non e fuggito."*
>   "It is not gone," Metastasio
> Is right—we have that world about us . . .
>   ["Canto I," *Poetry,* June 1917, p. 118]

Puvis is the nineteenth-century French painter, representative of the "half-light" in which the skeptical modern mind has to work as it attempts to convince itself that the world of the ambient gods is not gone.

> let's believe it . . .
>   . . . and shall I claim;
> Confuse my own phantastikon,
> Or say the filmy shell that circumscribes me
> Contains the actual sun;
>   confuse the thing I see
> With actual gods behind me?
>   Are they gods behind me?
>   ["Canto I," *Poetry,* June 1917, p. 120]

Pound had desired in *Poetry's* "Canto I" to resurrect a reverence for the religious imagination of past contexts.

> How shall we start hence, how begin the progress? . . .
>   With Egypt!
> Daub out in blue of scarabs, and with that greeny turquoise?
> Or with China, O *Virgilio mio,* and gray gradual steps
> Lead up beneath flat sprays of heavy cedars,
> Temple of teak wood . . .
>   [p. 119]

The *"Virgilio mio"* is addressed to Browning; the willingness to start with the blue-greens of Egyptian religious objects or the gray steps of the approach to a Chinese temple conveys both a sophistication and a respect for all ritual with commitment to none, which is the characteristic Poundian tonality. The lines are conflated in the final Canto 3 to "Green veins in the turquoise, / Or, the gray steps lead up under the cedars" (3/11:15). The aesthetic facts in a given ritual are substituted for the poet's earlier ambivalence toward any given ritual and its gods. That is, whatever the truth in a given ritual, the beauty, the quietude it produces is "World enough." The "gray steps" figure occurs throughout *The Cantos* as an image for the quietude, the "stillness," of ritual in a world whose true dynamic seems to be tumult and change.

The central image about which Canto 4 revolves is of a thin film of light over black water, representing the consolations of (crystal) vision counterpointed against human tragedy. Image clusters, conflations from mythological and lyric texts of the past, provide the fragile instances.

> Thus the light rains, thus pours, *e lo soleils plovil*
> The liquid and rushing crystal
>   beneath the knees of the gods.
> Ply over ply, thin glitter of water;
> Brook film bearing white petals . . .
>   Ply over ply
> The shallow eddying fluid,
>   beneath the knees of the gods.
>   [4/15:19]

Mountains (knees of the gods) are mythologized as gods dispensing blessed crystal streams (poetic visions) to the sensitive man; poets (Ovid, Vidal, Cabestan) keep experiencing life as dualistic and so create (ply over ply) myths (of Tereus, Actaeon, Cygnus, Persephone, Danaë) of vision/destruction, or of the endless waiting and watching (Danaë, and "we") in tragic circumstances for vision.

> Cabestan, Tereus,
>> It is Cabestan's heart in the dish,
> Vidal, or Ecbatan, upon the gilded tower in Ecbatan
> Lay the god's bride, lay ever, waiting the golden rain.
> And we sit here . . .
>> there in the arena . . .

> [4/16:20]

The mind's light (mirror) can look at the stones of destruction, "Troy but a heap of smouldering boundary stones" (4/13:17), and create a vision (much like the vision of the gods in the trees of Canto 3) in the "dew-haze" (the mind's "sheath").

> The silver mirrors catch the bright stones and flare,
> Dawn, to our waking, drifts in the green cool light;
> Dew-haze blurs, in the grass, pale ankles moving.
> Beat, beat, whirr, thud, in the soft turf
>> under the apple trees,
> Choros nympharum . . .

"Mirrors" is plural because it represents all poets' imaginings of, say, the ur-myth of Troy. Or in another figuration of the mind's light:

> The valley is thick with leaves, with leaves, the trees,
> The sunlight glitters, glitters a-top . . .
>> Beneath it, beneath it
> Not a ray, not a slivver, not a spare disc of sunlight
> Flaking the black, soft water

There in the darkness of woods comes to Actaeon the vision of Diana, "and the air, air, / Shaking, air alight with the goddess."

In the darkness of every sensitive sailor (in us, poets and observers) is the desire for the visionary moment's experience.

> The bark scrapes at the ford,
> Gilt rafters above black water,
> Three steps in an open field,
> Gray stone-posts leading . . .

One recognizes here a recurrent motif in *The Cantos:* the poet as
Odyssean sailor reaching in semidarkness a place lit by flares,
and preparing to continue his journey by foot (cf. Canto 17).
The gray stone posts recall the gray steps to the Oriental shrine
in Canto 3; the gilt rafters, also in Canto 3, evoke a
Mediterranean pagan temple, either ancient or Renaissance.
Canto 4 was published in the *Dial* in June 1920, and there the
last line of the passage ended thus: "Grey stone-posts leading
nowhither" (p. 691). Danaë's waiting leads ultimately nowhither,
Vidal's and Actaeon's vision likewise, for all "petals," things of
beauty, end floating in the water or cast on the stone. No wind
is the "King's" or anyone else's. Whether one worships at
Takasago, Ise, Mt. Rokku, or Santo Stefano, all one is sure of
obtaining from worship is the moment in beauty, the "thin film
of images"—such as, for instance, the frescoes on Santo Stefano's
wall. In the words of the *Dial* version,

> The vitreous fragile images
> Thin as the locust's wing
> Haunting the mind . . .

> [p. 692]

"Vitreous" as fragile glassware of porcelain or crystal, but also
as water flowing, as glint of light on dark water, caught in the
object of art.[1]

Canto 5 contrasts, first, Danaë waiting for the god's touch,
or vision, with the "daily-life-in-time" beneath her tower-prison,
and then the sparks, lights, of neo-Platonic and Dantesque
imagination with a sordid murder of Renaissance times (times
when neo-Platonism flourished again). Somewhere in between

the realm of the neo-Platonic Nous (or Dante's Empyream or Tenth Heaven) and the "hell-in-time," which so much of *The Cantos* dramatizes, is Pound's position, "Ego, Scriptor Cantilenae."

> Topaz I manage, and three sorts of blue;
>   but on the barb of time.
> The fire? always, and the vision always,
> Ear dull, perhaps, with the vision, flitting
> And fading at will.
>
> [5/17:21]

Pound's visions, therefore, are limited to the "diaphans" of sky blue and sea blue; his soul cannot ascend to a timeless realm. The opening line of the passage is reminiscent of lines in an earlier poem where Pound spoke to his "soul."

> Will we not find some headland consecrated
> By aery apostles of terrene delight,
> Will not our cult be founded on the waves,
> Clear sapphire, cobalt, cyanine,
> On triune azures, the impalpable
> Mirrors unstill of the eternal change?
>
> [Blandula, Tenulla, Vagula]

The religious language, especially the trinity of the "triune azures," is carefully poised. The self-delighting imagination creates its own perishable gods. "Triune azures" are not the white light of eternity, and the azure visions flit and fade, reflecting reality's eternal change. Pound aligns himself not with the neo-Platonists (*vide* his attitude toward them in *Poetry*'s "Canto III" and in the chapter on "Neo-Platonicks, etc." in *Guide to Kulchur*), but with the non-transcendental dramatists of the dualistic human condition, with poets like Sappho, whose words Pound quotes in this passage:

> Fades the light from the sea, and many things
> "Are set abroad and brought to mind of thee,"

And the vinestocks lie untended, new leaves come to the shoots,
North wind nips on the bough, and seas in heart
Toss up chill crests

[5/18:22]

"Light," "new leaves," "mind," and the "heart" are poised against
"fades," "untended," "North wind," and "chill crests" ("sea
change, a grey in the water," p. 18:22). Time pierces vision, as
in the death episodes of Agamemnon, Alessandro, and Mozarello
dramatized in the canto. Such counterbalancing of opposing
words and images is characteristic of Pound, and creates the
omnipresent dualistic tonality of The Cantos. It is important to
establish and to stress the presence of this tonality in these early,
much-discussed cantos, for they, as Pound said, "prepare the
palette."

As with the descriptions of historical personages who come
to a bad end in Canto 5, Canto 6 revolves around the sometimes
sordid, sometimes triumphant details in the lives of Guillaume
of Aquitaine, Eleanor, Cunizza (and, to come in Canto 8,
Sigismundo), and of the Provençal poets Daniel, Ventadour,
Sordello, Cairels, and Theseus. These people are distinguished
from ordinary malefactors in that they have created something
good (a gold thread in the weave) in art or society. The
achievements of Guillaume are expressed in language with
overtones of magic and myth. "The stone is alive in my hand,
the crops / will be thick in my death-year . . . ." (p. 21:25).
Animals out of air, using the Bacchus myth, in Canto 2, here
life out of stone, fertility out of death, using the Adonis myth
(cf. Canto 47), are variations on the recurring theme of the
"magic" of the artist or, more generally, of the creative
imagination. The original Dial version (August 1921) of Canto 6
includes other historical figures ("Conrad, the wheel turns and in
the end turns ill") and other poets ("En Bertrans cantat") to the
same effect—personages and poets all come to a bad end; their
achievements survive.

But barely. Pound sees himself in Canto 7 as one of those seeking for "buried beauty"; the forgotten muses are mourned for; the true museums of cultured minds where all good art is contemporaneous are, in the early twentieth century, "lost," "burned," or compartmentalized by stiff, professorial old men who dominate the cultural scene (cf. the "old men's voices" of Canto 2):

> Shell of the older house,
> Brown-yellow wood, and the no colour plaster,
> Dry professorial talk . . .
> > now stilling the ill beat music,
> House expulsed by this house.

[7/26:30]

Pound cannot abide the modern situation as he sees it; he, "stubborn against the fact," will "seek the living," which are dead artists' works "more live than they," the professors. He will, in so doing, break the false "partitions," false distinctions, and false categories of the contemporary (around 1910) house of criticism that has warped the history of literature from Homer to Henry James. The professors feel they deal with "fact" or "Truth"; they are, however, without the creative "flame" that "leaps from the hand." The great artists of the past (including Flaubert and Daniel) have had the "thirst," the "passion to breed a form in shimmer of rain-blur," as Pound does in his image of Nicea in London.

> And all that day
> Nicea moved before me
> And the cold grey air troubled her not
> For all her naked beauty, bit not the tropic skin,
> And the long slender feet lit on the curb's marge
> And her moving height went before me,
> > We alone having being.

[7/26:30]

This introduction of the lyric mode in a canto of sophisticated social and aesthetic commentary, and the near comedy of the handling (London damp on tropic skin, lyric feet on London curb), emphasizes again the complex, ambivalent tonality reflexive in the modern poet who wants to assert the primacy of the lyric impulse, of subjective Beauty, over contemporary Truth.[2]

> These fragments you have shelved (shored).
> "Slut!" "Bitch!" Truth and Calliope
> Slanging each other sous les lauriers [under the laurels]:
> *That* Alessandro was negroid. And Malatesta
> Sigismund:
>
> [8/28:32]

Fragments of beauty, moments of vision, imaged in Canto 7 among the "beer bottles" of our time, are what the poet has shored up against the modern "wasteland." In, as it were, a medieval poetic competition of poets insulting each other, "Truth" mentions that *maugre* poetic license, the negroid Alessandro de Medici cannot be called "biondo" (blond) as he was called at the end of Canto 7.

No more than Sigismundo de Malatesta, who built the great Tempio, can be called "good" or "moral." It is, in fact, now Pound's self-imposed task in Cantos 8-11 to create precise definitions, which will turn out to be images, by creating the precise dualistic contexts in which Malatesta's achievements must be understood (the same intention operative in the Chinese and the Adams cantos, 52-71). The whole effect of these cantos of laborious detailing seems intended to represent the always difficult struggle to distinguish, separate, and maintain the good in the historical process (the gold in the gloom), whether it be economic, social, or artistic. The function of the few interspersed passages in the lyric mood or mode in these four cantos is to dramatize the fragile, temporary nature of the victories in the struggle (wind), which is an eternal struggle.

> He, Sigismundo, *templum aedificavit...*
> And the wind is still for a little
> And the dusk rolled
>   to one side a little . . .

[8/32:36]

> And we sit here. I have sat here
>   For forty four thousand years.

[11/50:54]

Canto 12, like Canto 7, though in a more vulgar arena, demonstrates evils modern yet thousands of years old ("and we sit here", p. 53:57), the antisocial effects of the usurious temperament. Canto 13 then demonstrates the finest social intelligence Pound feels the world has yet seen in the Confucian order. The canto itself is self-explanatory. I would only comment that Pound, in drawing his model early, is clearly not intending *The Cantos* to move toward a "culminating" definition or vision of any specific "city of Dioce" (p. 425:451) or particular "paradise terrestre" (p. 802:32). Earthly paradises for Pound are various and have come and gone, for they are effective spiritual or social contexts gained at points of time. A deadening effect in the literature on *The Cantos* has been that various critics, perhaps taking some comments of Pound too literally, are always waiting for the one culminating vision, crystal, or paradise, while Pound is at pains always to tell us that the Nous, or knowledge of a transcendent reality, is not accessible. For man there are only the intermittent moments. "The blossoms of the apricot / blow from the east to the west, / And I have tried to keep them from falling" (p. 60:64). The poignant paradoxes in these final Confucian lines from Canto 13, the realization that no social order can endure, ought to make clear that the placing of this canto between two versions of an earthly hell in Cantos 12 and 14 is not slapdash but intentional, to balance as he has been doing all along in his syntax, vocabulary, and his image complexes, mud and light, gold and gloom, intermittent heavens in recurring hells.

Cantos 14–16 wittily and bawdily create a hell for obstructors of social orders and then end with (1) an allegory of ascent into the purgatory that is the real world of action, frustration, and achievement, (2) a symbolic description of the mind's "moments" of light "outside" of Time, and finally, (3) a coda to the first sixteen cantos that returns poet and readers to the world of war and usury always there to combat achievement or social order.

> Andiamo! . . .
> and again Plotinus:
>   To the door,
> Keep your eyes on the mirror.
> Prayed we to the Medusa,
>   petrifying the soil by the shield
> Holding it downward
>   he hardened the track . . .
> Half the width of a sword's edge.
>   By this through the dern evil,
> now sinking, now clinging,
>   Holding the unsinkable shield.
>
>   [15/66:70]

One hesitates to call the passage or the whole context visionary; sophisticated, often self-ironic, highly conscious allegory is really the mode. In any case, these cantos include or introduce in this deliberate way many motifs that are used in passages descriptive of psychic moments elsewhere in *The Cantos* and are important, therefore, to the analysis of the lyric patterns.

Plotinus saying "Andiamo" is meant to set the arch tonality. The Medusa is a fearful monster, but it is apt here to pray to her—for some people, society's obstructors, and some bog-land, decaying societies, deserve to be turned to stone. Perseus, in the myth (cf. Ovid's *Metamorphoses,* Loeb ed.,

IV:605), avoided such a fate by not facing the monster directly
but through her reflection in his shield. The poet is cautioned in
the canto passage to keep his eyes on the "mirror" (his
"shield's" surface) and head toward the "door," or "gate," into
the light, the "path" being "half the width of a sword's edge."
This last detail (a recurring motif), in particular, should make it
clear that what we have in the canto is an allegory of a mind's
journey. The mind of the poet finds release in this allegory
through its own "light" (his shield, his mirror, as distinguished
in Canto 16/68:72 from those of others, such as Plotinus, Dante,
Sordello, who also have the creative flame).

> Oblivion,
>   forget how long
> sleep, fainting nausea.
>   "Whether in Naishapur or Babylon"
> I heard in the dream.
>   Plotinus gone,
> And the shield tied under me, woke;
> The gate swung on its hinges . . .
>
>   [15/66:70]

The burden of the lyric in the dream is of transience; it is an
allusion to the *Rubáiyát*.

> Whether at Naishapur or Babylon
> Whether the Cup with sweet or bitter run,
> The Wine of Life keeps oozing drop by drop,
> The Leaves of Life keep falling one by one.
>
>   [Fitzgerald trans., verse XIII]

The door or gate motif recurs often in *The Cantos* (pp. 77:81,
236–38:246–48) bringing one to a mind's place better than
where the mind has been. Pound's lyric places are full of blessed
mountains with holy temples at their peaks and holy caves at
their bases (pp. 69:73, 76:80, 90:94). But there are also the
"steel" mountains of the hell psyche of Cantos 14–15. It is the

poet's business to "circumnavigate," or "climb" or "enter into" the mountains, to illuminate and sanctify them with the mind's light (one's "shield" or "mirror"), which job philosophers and poets like Plotinus, Augustine, Pierre Cardinal, Sordello, Dante, and Blake have done according to their lights.

> Il Fiorentino,
> Seeing hell in his mirror,
>   and lo Sordels
> Looking on it in his shield;
> And Augustine, gazing toward the invisible
>
> [16/68:72]

But it is not up to a transcendental reality that the modern poet of Pound's consciousness must go (as with Plotinus, Augustine, and Dante) but down, a descent into the mind's own light.

> The grey stone posts,
>   and the stair of gray stone,
> the passage clean squared in granite:
>   descending,
> and I through this, and into the earth,
>   patet terra,
> entered the quiet air
>   the new sky,
> the light as after a sun-set,
>
> [16/69:73]

We have seen the gray stone posts and stair images before (Cantos 3 and 4). We will see again the motif of entering into a "cave" (Canto 17) or "mountain" (Canto 47) or, as here, new place, where the light is "as after a sun-set." That is, the light is "not of the sun" (Canto 17) but of the creative imagination. It is in that private place where the "heroes" gaze at "the mounts of their cities," their dreams, and weave their "water reeds." One cannot overemphasize, I think, the poignancy of this lyric image of the fragility of the heroes' achievements.

Pound has traveled to this place and dreams now, at the end of Canto 16, of the horrors of the place he has left. Canto 17 and other passages in the next volume of cantos to be published describe again in new lyric terms the psychic places the poet's mind achieves.

# 3: CANTOS 17-30

C antos 17–27 were published in 1928 in a
limited edition similar to *A Draft of XVI
Cantos*. In 1930 *A Draft of XXX Cantos* appeared in a limited
edition produced in Paris, followed in 1933 by trade editions
produced in America and England. These fourteen cantos
contain a varied group of heroes and anti-heroes in the world of
action and are punctuated by a series of interconnected lyric
passages clearly related to and developing out of the visionary
imagery of the preceding cantos. The dominant image is that of
men of "craft," doers, in silver-beaked boats that catch
moonlight, sailing on black water to their private places of
dreams, visions of cities and temples to build, artistic and social
gardens to cultivate. The traveler ultimately approaches his place
by stream or path, entering valleys, mountains, or caves. Some

are sailing, some walking, some resting by fountains; all take
spiritual nourishment denied to the souls of the impenetrable
Tovarisches who can never respond to what they feel are the
outmoded fantasies of the imagination:

> And the sun lay over the wind,
> And three forms became in the air
> And hovered about him,
> > so that he said;
> This machinery is very ancient,
> > surely we have heard this before.
> And the waves like a forest
> Where the wind is weightless in the leaves
> But moving,
> > so that the sound runs upon sound.
> > Xarites, born of Venus and wine.
> Carved stone upon stone,
> But in sleep, in the waking dream,
> Petal'd the air;
> > twig where but wind-streak had been;
> Moving bough without root,
> > > by Helios
> So that the Xarites bent over Tovarisch

> > > > [27/131:136]

The Graces cannot move Tovarisch, mass man of revolutions; he
sees the imagination's creations, forms, forests in the mind's air
(cf. the animals out of air of Canto 2), as but machinery. He
could never understand the psychic experience Pound is at pains
to describe in "The Tree," a very early poem—"I stood still and
was a tree amid the wood"—or the similar effect which begins
Canto 17: "So that the vines burst from my fingers." The "so
that" beginning the canto is to emphasize that the efforts of the
creative imagination are indeed an effect of the pressures of
reality, as they are described in the preceding cantos. The
imagery of "cities set in their hills" in the opening lines of the
canto is meant to link with the lyric landscape of Canto 16:

> . . . founders, gazing at the mounts of their cities.
> The plain, distance, and in fount-pools
>   the nymphs of that water
> rising, spreading their garlands,
>   weaving their water reeds with the boughs,
> In the quiet,
>   and now one man rose from his fountain
> and went off into the plain.
>
> [16/69:73]

The "one man" reappears in Canto 17 and speaks; his speech,
his vision, is representative of all men who come to the blessed
land of whatever one "lov'st well," the place of personal vision
which each man builds ("carves") from his own materials.

> Flat water before me,
>   and the trees growing in water,
> Marble trunks out of stillness,
> On past the palazzi,
>   in the stillness,
> The light now, not of the sun.
>
> [p. 76:80]

Pound emphasizes in the "flat water" the *ex nihilo* aspect (cf.
the transformations "out of nothing" in Canto 2) of the
achievement; the recurrent motif of marble trunks "growing"
out of the water (i.e., with no foundation) functions similarly.[1]
The mind's moments (in the "cave of Nerea") are thus true
neither to nature ("not of the sun," cf. the "grapes without
seed" of Canto 2) nor to a transcendental absolute, but to the
mind's own need to make life (sculpture, architecture) out of
dead stone.

>   A boat came,
> One man holding her sail,
> Guiding her with oar caught over gunwale, saying:
> "   There, in the forest of marble,
> "   the stone trees—out of water—

> "   . . . silver beaks rising and crossing,
> "   prow set against prow,
> "   stone, ply over ply,
> "   the gilt beams flare of an evening"
> Borso, Carmagnola, the men of craft, *i vitrei,*
> Thither, at one time, time after time,
> And the waters richer than glass . . .
>
> [p. 77:81]

Creative people and men of worthy action keep sailing to these
rich waters throughout human history (the "ply after ply"
motif). The gilt beams that flare of an evening we have seen
before in Cantos 3 and 4, and they represent the recurring idea
of small light in great gloom (cf. the "dye pots" and "torch
light" in Cantos 17 and 47 and elsewhere). All creative men are
makers of "glass" or "crystal," of fragile achievements, of
moments of calm in troubled lives.

> "For this hour, brother of Circe."
> Arm laid over my shoulder,
> Saw the sun for three days . . .
>   and that day,
> And for three days, and none after,
> Splendour . . .
>
> [p. 79:83]

The mythological reference is presumably to the river god
Acheleus, brother of Circe, being spoken to perhaps by Theseus,
who takes a respite from his labors at Acheleus's feast (see
Ovid's *Metamorphoses,* Loeb ed., VIII:48-72). Theseus's arm on
the poet's shoulder could as well be Borso's or Sigismundo's,
brothers all, who have fought, won, and lost, and are "thence"
shipped "thither," to the "gray light" of the "stone place." The
poet's light is here, as always, enveloped in darkness, "light as
after a sunset" (Canto 16), and transitory, "Sunset like the
grasshopper flying" (p. 79:83). The goddesses (Athene and
Kore) and ladies (Zother and Aletha) are observers (cf. the
motif "and we sit here, there, in the arena"), looking out on the

gray landscape at the ships entering and moving about. Their
eyes are ever "seaward," and they are cognizant of things like
"sea-wrack," "dust," and "salt" (cf. the later motif, pp. 195:203,
435:462, of the goddess's "stone eyes looking seaward" on to an
equally dualistic scene). Each man enters (via "gate cliffs") his
own place ("one cut," "valley," or "alley"), to an inner cave and
"suavity of the rock", "no cold there." "Suave" is used
throughout *The Cantos* (cf. p. 425:451), first to denote the
constant laving of rock by water and also, more importantly, to
connote the sophisticated pleasures of the imagination in its
haven. Gods are there, Zagreus (Dionysus-Bacchus of Canto 2)
with his leopards, and others (cf. Canto 3, "Gods float in the
azure air"). The experience in the cave of Nerea, in "that place"
(p. 90:94), is, as always in Pound, intermittent, trembling as
light trembles, the black sea always returning to the
consciousness: "Beyond, sea, . . . / Night sea churning
shingle . . ." (p. 77:81).

　　Canto 17, in its distillation of motifs recurring throughout
this group of cantos and the whole poem, is central and
illuminating (perhaps no canto more so, save for Canto 2), and
especially so in untangling the apparent confusions in Canto 20.

> In the sunlight, gate cut by the shadow;
> And then the faceted air;
> Floating. Below, sea churning shingle.
> Floating, each on invisible raft,
> On the high current, invisible fluid,
> Borne over the plain . . .
> Each man in his cloth, as on raft, on
> 　　　The high invisible current;
> On toward the fall of water;
> And then over that cataract . . .
>
> 　　　　　　　　　　　　　　　　[20/92:96]

The image of each man on his own ("invisible") raft moving
toward the cataract of death is reminiscent not only of the
heroes in ships of Canto 17 but also of:

When, when, and whenever death closes our eyelids,
Moving naked over Acheron
Upon the one raft, victor and conquered together,
Marius and Jugurtha together,
                              one tangle of shadows.
                              (*Homage to Sextus Propertius,* VI)

Each man, in the passage from Canto 20, is in his "cloth," or
"wrapped" in his "burnous," representing each man's fashion or
mode of seeing (cf. the "sheath" image discussed earlier and the
later motif, in Canto 95, of the poet as Ulysses on a raft, saved
from drowning by Leucothea's "scarf" or "Kredemnon"). The
"gate" represents, as mentioned earlier, the doors of imaginative
perception; the empty air (cf. "void air" in 2/8:12) is
"faceted" when the mind populates it with crystal visions.

The canto deals with differing *façons de voir* of mankind
locked in the current, of Saint Francis ("In the fire of love He
put me") first, and then of others.

Or followed the water. Or looked back to the flowing;
Others approaching that cataract . . .
And from the floating bodies, the incense
      blue-pale, purple above them.
Shelf of the lotophagoi,
Aerial, cut in the aether . . .
                        "Feared neither death nor pain for this beauty;
If harm, harm to ourselves."
And beneath: the clear bones, far down,
Thousand on thousand.

                                        [p. 93:97]

It is important for a sense of the whole canto to note that the
lotophagoi passage proper is short and is preceded by one (the
first two lines of the passage) on mere observers and succeeded
by one (introduced in the last two lines) on the "Thousand on
thousand" who, below the aerial shelf of the lotophagoi,
complain justly and at length of their fate. The former and the
latter are not lotophagoi types but represent eternal crewmen
who eternally take nothing. The extended allegory of a trip to a

cliff under rock into "inner roadside," with which the canto ends is, then, but one more (the "and . . . and" motif) response to the rushing toward death of the river of life.

> And from the plain whence the water-shoot,
> Across, back, to the right, the roads, a way in the grass,
> The Khan's hunting leopard, and young Salustio
> And Ixotta; the suave turf
> Ac ferae familiares, and the cars slowly,
> And the panthers, soft-footed.
> Plain, as the plain of Somnus . . .
>
> [p. 94:98]

The "plain of Somnus" phrase makes it clear that this particular allegoric journey inside the "mountain" and to an end point of the journey is, in Pound's view, a wrongish path (though not absurdly wrong, as the lotophagoi are not absurdly wrong). One finds on this "plain" by the river's course the "Khan's hunting leopard" (the Khan's vision of mastery) and Sigismundo's beloved Ixotta with the child Salustio (Malatesta's vision). Leitmotifs of lyric passages that we have met with before (cf. Canto 17) are here: leopards, panthers, the rock cliff, the suavity, the soundlessness. The details not recurrent are those specific, as Hugh Kenner sees it, to baroque art. They culminate in the vision of the lady Vanoka:

> And at last, between gilded barocco,
> Two columns coiled and fluted,
> Vanoka, leaning half naked,
>   waste hall there behind her.
>
> [p. 95:99]

One senses that the allegoric passage exists as a commentary of Pound's, using his visionary or lyric mode, on the insufficiency of the baroque "way of seeing" in art and life. The entire Canto 20 is, in fact, a series of descriptions of ways of seeing, some better (St. Francis's) than others (baroque).[2]

The canto opens (much as Canto 7 opened) with a cryptic meditation on lyricism ("almond trees flowering") from Homer

through Ovid and Propertius to the poets of Provence. The
Provençal way of seeing is then given an especially beautiful
lyric rendering:

> Wind over the olive trees, ranunculae ordered,
> By the clear edge of the rocks
> The water runs, and the wind scented with pine
> And with hay-fields under sun-swath.
> Agostino, Jacopo and Boccata.
> You would be happy for the smell of that place
> And never tired of being there, either alone
> Or accompanied.
> Sound: as of the nightingale too far off to be heard.
> Sandro, and Boccata, and Jacopo Sellaio;
> The ranunculae, and almond,
> Boughs set in espalier,
> Duccio, Agostino; e l'olors—
> The smell of that place—d'enoi ganres.
> Air moving under the boughs,
> The cedars there in the sun,
> Hay new cut on hill slope,
> And the water there in the cut
> Between the two lower meadows; sound,
> The sound, as I have said, a nightingale
> Too far off to be heard.
> And the light falls, remir,
> From her breast to thighs.

[p. 90:94]

This description of "that place," soundless as other visionary
places in *The Cantos*, is full of the imagery and light of the
Provençal imagination that feminizes nature—hills and valley
seen as the lady's breasts and thighs—a way of seeing that
inspired artists of early Italy, and still inspires old Lévy and
Pound.

Out of the myriad perceptions of humanity (the "jungle"),
some few have lasting worth ("clear shapes"), and, Pound muses,
it may be that the poetic or creative eye is allowed broken,
disrupted glimpses of the "body eternal," a higher transcendent,

ideal reality. Whether so or not, poetic visions are what we have
of paradise ("God's eye art'ou, do not surrender perception," p.
790:20).

> . . . jungle,
> Basis of renewal, renewals;
> Rising over the soul, green virid, of the jungle,
> Lozenge of the pavement, clear shapes,
> Broken, disrupted, body eternal,
> Wilderness of renewals, confusion
> Basis of renewals, subsistence
>
> [p. 91:95]

This motif is picked up in Canto 21: "In the crisp air, / the
discontinuous gods; / . . . confusion; / Confusion, source of
renewals (p. 99:103). The "clear shapes," the "crisp air," set in
contrast to "wilderness" and "confusion," develop an idea
central to *The Cantos*.[3] The ideal is of an attained clarity, sharp
sculptural cut, sharp edge of bough against the sky or cliff
against sea, of a temporarily achieved crystal clarity against the
inevitable return of mist, ignorance, confusion, and chaos:

> And there was grass on the floor of the temple,
> Or where the floor of it might have been;
> Gold fades in the gloom . . .
> . . . and we sit here
> By the arena, *les gradins* . . .
>
> [21/98:102]

The "steps" lead, as they usually do in *The Cantos,* to a new
vision or version (here to the "Heliads" dancing) of "that place,"
"that hour":

> steps, cut in the basalt.
> Danced there Athame, danced, and there Phaethusa
> With colour in the vein
>
> [p. 100:104]

Canto 21 keeps creating examples (here in the floating
Venetianesque city imagery we had experienced in Canto 17) of
the mind's temporary conquering of gloom and darkness:

And the palazzo, baseless, hangs there in the dawn
With low mist over the tide-mark;
And floats there nel tramonto [in the sunset]
With gold mist over the tide-mark.

[p. 98:102]

and of beauty born ("Gignetei Kalon") out of the "dry black of
the night." Voices, flashes, flames, become clear in the
temporary, beautiful valley "under the day's edge," in the light
"not of the sun."

And now in the valley,
Valley under the day's edge: . . .
And the boughs cut on the air . . .
           water still black in the shadow.
In the crisp air,
       The discontinuous gods

[p. 99:103]

The whole context underscores again the dualism at the center
of Pound's vision; voices grow "faint," light "fades," color
"pales." The gods come (Apollo or the Virgin) in the psychic
moment, they are gone once out of the psychic moment, and
neither the having nor the not having is to be falsified. The
moment is as "impenetrable as the ignorance of old women."
The ironic tone of the last comparison is maintained in the
cryptic allusion a few lines later in the canto to the story of
Tmolus (Ovid's *Metamorphoses,* Loeb ed., XI:145–93), who
punished foolish King Midas with donkey's ears for preferring
Pan's music to Apollo's. To scoff at the exalted lyric mood, at
gods and visions, because one doesn't experience it is to be a
Midas or, in modern terms, a Tovarisch. The canto's "old man"
(sad representative of Tmolus) has only one club against the
stubborn beast, as has any lyric art against skepticism, and that
is the "asphodel," a flower, symbol of fragile beauty (also
etymologically, in Greek, king's spear).

The poignancy of the struggle of the artist's vision versus
Tovarisch's is that of the "flute" versus "Phlegethon" (river of

hell or Erebus) in the great culminating lyric of Canto 25; hell, "that bolge," in this instance a once-vital society, now decayed, Heaven, the society whose rituals and gods still have vitality.

> And as after the form, the shadow,
> Noble forms, lacking life, that bolge, that valley
> the dead words keeping form,
> and the cry: Civis Romanus.
> The clear air, dark, dark,
> The dead concepts, never the solid, the blood rite,
> The vanity of Ferrara;
>
> Clearer than shades, in the hill road
> Springing in cleft of the rock: Phaethusa
> There as she came among them,
> Wine in the smoke-faint throat,
> Fire gleam under smoke of the mountain,
> Even there by meadows of Phlegethon
>
> And against this the flute: pone metum.
> Fading, that they carried their guts before them,
> And thought then, the deathless,
> Form, forms and renewal, gods held in the air,
> Forms seen, and then clearness,
> Bright void, without image, Napishtim,
> Casting his gods back into the νοῦς.
>
> [25/118:123]

The "flute" that allays fear ("pone metum") is the form seen, made manifest to the imaginative perception and crystallized into an artistic image ("music," "harmony," the "gods") or social order. All one knows is that the form is seen, felt, and then its loss is felt. One is left with "clearness, / Bright void, without image," a "clearness" quite the opposite of the clearness of the image of a Phaethusa dancing and offering wine in a hill-cleft (cf. the last lines of Canto 21). Whatever the ontological status of the aesthetic form or the vision of "gods," or of the Platonic "forma" or "concetto" they may imply, or of the higher reality or "Nous" beyond, it is the business of the passage (and of *The Cantos*) to dramatize the sense of both their

perishability and their imperishability in the subjective mind of
the poetic temperament.[4] Social orders and gods have their day,
and then they decay, fade into mist, smoke, shade; the gods of
Napishtim (of the ancient *Gilgamesh* epic) have become "dead
concepts," but the visions of the gods return in different forms
(perhaps from humanity's will to believe), as a new vision of
Aphrodite to a new Anchises:

> and saw then, as of waves taking form,
> As the sea, hard, a glitter of crystal,
> And the waves rising but formed, holding their form.
> No light reaching through them.

[23/109:114]

> and saw the waves taking form as crystal
> notes as facets of air,
> and the mind there, before them, moving,
> so that notes needed not move.

[25/119:124]

It needs to be stressed, concerning this recurrent motif, that the
crystal vision is a fixing of waves; no amount of discussion of
how crystals are formed from water can obviate the equally
present connotations of the mind's impossible desire to order
the sea, to fix the flow or, in the earlier Confucian image, "to
keep the blossoms from falling" ("notes as facets of air"
embodies the same ambiguity). Central, too, to Pound's cast of
mind are the implications of the phrase "no light reaching
through them." The crystal vision, or the moment, is absolutely
its own place, while the Anchises figure, or the poet, sculptor, is
in the moment. It is a light "not of the sun" but of the mind,
which moves with change (wave motion) not because it wants to
but because it must. A new time brings a new poetry.

> Mist gone.
>   And Sulpicia
> green shoot now, and the wood
> white under new cortex

[25/117:122]

Sulpicia, the Roman love poetess, is, of course, a "green shoot"
no longer, but it is as Canto 95 says, "love, gone as lightning,/
enduring 5000 years" (p. 643:676). Sulpicia's "flute" is
twig-strong, but she can say of one day in her life "Hic mihi dies
sanctus" ("This day is holy for me"), as is said about "this hour"
or "this place" by poets and other people of accomplishment
throughout *The Cantos* about their crystal moments of vision,
or "music."

Canto 23 begins with a pastiche of examples of such
adventurers of the spirit, people Pound admires—Psellos,
Gemisto, Malatesta, the Curies, Pierre de Maensac, "my brother"
—and some who, like Pound, wrestle with the difficulties of an
ancient text for the right reasons. In the midst of these examples
is a passage in the lyric mode which represents the temporary
havens that such adventurers win.

>   And the rose grown while I slept,
>   And the strings shaken with music,
>   Capriped, the loose twigs under foot;
>   We here on the hill, with the olives
>   Where a man might carry his oar up,
>   And the boat there in the inlet . . .
>   As we had stood there,
>   Watching road from the window,
>   Fa Han and I at the window . . .
>   dawn-branch in the sky
>   And the sea dark, under wind,
>   The boat's sails hung loose at the mooring,
>   Cloud like a sail inverted,
>   And the men dumping sand by the sea-wall
>   Olive trees there on the hill
>   where a man might carry his oar up.
>
> [23/108:112]

We are again at "that place" where each "voyager" comes at
times, where on a hill loved by the perceptive eye one can rest
and look down on men shoring up levees, cultivating fields, see
the dawn and the dark and the sail's reflection in the sea, a place

of stillness. John Peck in *Paideuma* 3:1:64 glosses Fa Han as han² fa³·⁵ "bound hair" (Mathew's dictionary 1770.19); she is one more fair-tressed lady of Pound's visionary landscapes.⁵ This, then, is one more set of images to represent, in lyric terms, the state of mind represented elsewhere by images of a raft on a river, a cart "entering" a mountain or cave, stairs into the earth, a hayfield on a hill slope, a boat entering a "forest of marble," or a silver-prowed gondola entering the floating, Venetian-like city in the mist.

> And at night they sang in the gondolas
> And in the barche with lanthorns;
> The prows rose silver on silver
>   taking light in the darkness . . .
>
> [26/121:126]

> Glide of water, lights and the prore,
> Silver beaks out of night,
> Stone, bough over bough,
>   lamps fluid in water,
> Pine by the black trunk of its shadow . . .
> The trees melted in air.
>
> [29/146:151]

Whatever the setting, the mindscape, the one clear law of all these lights in the darkness, these visions, has been that they all are perishable; except in art, they all end "melted in air" (*vide* Prospero's poignant soliloquy in *The Tempest,* act 4, scene 1).

The quotation above from Canto 29 constitutes the last lines of the canto, a canto that up to this point had been primarily concerned with the incomprehensions of youth: the young man's ("lusty Juventus") arrogant confidence in his own abstractions and the girl's impossible-to-fulfill (and confused) desires. Their sexuality, too, is misunderstood; it is Pound's position, as I understand it, that the sexual life is a necessary but not sufficient ordering of life that can become destructive if it does not lead to a further aesthetic ordering. The theme of the possible destructiveness of sexual relations or, to be more

pointed, of a disordered woman stifling creative potential in a
poet, can be traced also through the *Personae* poems, as in
"Portrait d'un Femme" and "Near Perigord," in the opening
lines of Canto 27, Madame Hyle in Canto 30, Circe in Canto 39.
The theme of the possible hell of sexual relations is not really
within the province of my subject;[6] within that province is the
artist's transformation of that hell into the heavenly lyric mood
figured in the ladies of the lyric passages in *The Cantos*. The
conscious attempt in Canto 29 is to balance the hell with the
heaven in the contrast between the satiric handling of the small
town, the limited, uncomprehending lovers ("Let us speak of the
osmosis of persons"), and the finale of the canto, where a
pastoral maiden is apotheosized into a paradisal lady. She is
placed in another landscape of mountain and stream, which is
another variation on the "mind's place," of "clear shapes," and
sharp-cut sculptural images.

> The cut cool of the air,
> Blossom cut on the wind, by Helios
> Lord of the Light's edge, and April
> Blown round the feet of the God,
> Beauty on an ass-cart
> Sitting on five sacks of laundry . . .
>   Eyes brown topaz,
> Brookwater over brown sand,
> The white hounds on the slope,
> Glide of water, lights and the prore,
> Silver beaks out of night, . . .

                                    [29/145:150]

The canto is one more variation on the twin themes of Erebus
and the lady, of reality and vision, truth and beauty, evident
from the beginning of Pound's work—hell, in this instance, being
the social and sexual relations of the quotidian, the lady what
she always is, the blessed, creative escape from the quotidian.

4: THE CANTOS
OF THE THIRTIES

E*leven New Cantos XXXI–XLI* appeared in
1934, *The Fifth Decade of Cantos* in 1937,
and *Cantos LII–LXXI* in early 1940. Written in Italy, these
forty-one cantos are almost double the bulk of the first thirty,
incorporating for long stretches the techniques of presentation
developed in the Malatesta Cantos 8–11. The length and point
of the 1940 volume's incantatory sketch of Chinese history and
the profile of John Adams via snatches from his journals,
particularly, have been called into question. I would hesitate to
label anything in Pound as uncontrolled rant or ramble; the
Chinese and Adams sections both seem to me to work on a
responsive reader's psychology in ways that Pound intended and
controlled. Various cultural heroes and anti-heroes are presented
in these cantos as in previous ones. As in my treatment of

previous cantos, I will consider these figures and other historical aspects of these cantos only in so far as they impinge on the imagery and substance of the lyric passages. There are fewer lyric passages in the cantos of the thirties and almost none in the 1940 volume. This ought not only to be seen, I feel, as evidence of a man simply obsessed with economic and social issues (though he was) but also of a cunning and confident artist who had long ago "prepared his palette" and is exhilarated by new experiments in audacious regions. The lyric cantos most closely linked with the imagery and themes in the lyric passages of the first thirty cantos are Cantos 39 and 47, and a major effort of this chapter will be to illuminate what is actually at the center of the body of attitudes in these clearly pivotal cantos.

The lyric moments do come less often in these cantos, but just as unpredictably and to the same purpose, which is clear to the reader in hindsight—to punctuate the long, and mostly unhappy, overview of man's condition in the world of experience with lyric meditation on the creative light in man's mind that inspires the new building, the new society, the new art. *Litterae nihil sanantes,* writes Thomas Jefferson in Canto 33, but that sobering truth of overview will not prevent Jefferson or any man of energy or artistry from trying to combine art and action, right thought with right action.

And so it need not appear capricious, or simply scrapbook technique here (or anywhere in *The Cantos*) that, say, Canto 35 on the "general indefinite wobble" of modern middle-European culture and on the Venetian descent into usury in the fifteenth century be followed by the free translation ("imitation" really) of Cavalcanti's lofty meditation on "Love," or that Canto 36 be followed by the canto on Van Buren, who had fought the good fight against usurious banking interests. A poignancy that the Cavalcanti does not itself have is created by its juxtapositioning between cantos of the world of action, where the beauty of thought is always polluted by the encroachment of the evils of men and time.

What we have in Canto 36 cannot, should not, be
considered so much Cavalcanti's poem but, instead, a liberal
using of the "Canzone" for Pound's purposes, an interpretation
of all the admitted cruxes one way, the way that is congenial to
the body of ideas *The Cantos* is developing throughout.
Pound's first translation of the "Canzone" in the twenties, and
the elaborate accompanying notes expressing his unsureness
concerning line after line, is a matter significantly different from
the canto version. It is the canto version's relation to *The Cantos*
as a whole that I want to make clear.[1]

> Wherefore I speak to the present knowers
> Having no hope that low-hearted
>   Can bring sight to such reason . . .
>
> Where memory liveth
>   it takes its state
> Formed like a diafan from light on shade . . .
>
> Cometh from a seen form which being understood
> Taketh locus and remaining in the intellect possible
> Wherein hath he neither weight nor still-standing . . .
>   [36/177:182]

Love ("he") takes "locus" (place) in the responsive minds of
those who have seen and felt ("'tis felt, I say"). Love is not
described as an absolute existing outside the mind but as a
subjective response to an objective ("seen" or "manifest") form.
Love having "neither weight nor still-standing," whatever the
original line in Cavalcanti means, is a recurring idea in Pound,
representing the ambiguous status, ontologically, of the loved
"diaphans" or "visions" of the creative imagination. Love is a
"diaphan," a "sheath," "haze," or "halo" that the mind casts
over an object of love out in the darkness. There may be an
absolute in a Platonic higher reality of which this diaphanous
love is but a shadow, but of this dimension (what Pound calls
"the NOUS, the ineffable crystal" in Canto 40), we can know
nothing. The positions here and much of the imagery are

those of both the great lyric of Canto 81 and of Canto 90 that
ushers in the extended meditations on love through Canto 95. It
becomes clear in a restudy of these later cantos that their
thought and their language is in large measure a recollection and
a development of the language of Canto 36.

> Cometh he to be
> > when the will
> From overplus
> Twisteth out of natural measure . . .
>
> And his strange quality sets sighs to move
> Willing man look into that formed trace in his mind
> And with such uneasiness as rouseth the flame.
> Unskilled can not form his image . . .

[p. 178:183]

"Out of erebus" (Canto 1), "out of nothing" (Canto 2) comes
the "forméd trace" in the mind, when the skilled artist (or
"knower") in his uneasiness rouses the "flame" that is the
creative imagination, that comes, that is, when the will desires
more than nature (the seen form, the manifest) supplies.
"Forméd trace" is in fact a willed phrase of Pound's for "in un
formato locho." His earlier translation had been "in unformed
space," based on the variant "non formato." He expresses his
reluctance to accept this variant in his notes in the Cavalcanti
essay. No detail is more telling to show the subtle choices of
language and emphasis that together make the canto passage
more Pound's than Cavalcanti's. Later in the passage "Beauty's
dart" pierces the poet's heart (pain in pleasure) because he
cannot know the divine face in the "white light that is allness";
he cannot, that is, see (Platonic) "form," but only
"emanations": "Disjunct in mid darkness / Grazeth the light,
. . ." (p. 179:184). Light represents for Pound in *The Cantos*
the creative intelligence in man's mind (whatever it may
represent for Cavalcanti, Grosseteste, Eriugena) that may or may
not have a transcendental source; the poet's position, however,

is always clear—disjunct in mid-darkness, he is grateful for the
touch of light and love, be it absolute light or subjective illusion.

The rest of Canto 36 is a cryptic documentation of Pound's
belief that men of rich thought, such as Scotus Eriugena and
Sordello, will always appear heretical or foolish to those who do
not understand. They, and others like them, occupy "thrones"
of honor in Pound's hierarchy (the allusion is to Dante's
Paradiso IX:66–69; the semi-precious gemstones balascio and
topaz represent rich thought that is less than divine knowledge,
as one moves in the *Paradiso* from lower to higher levels of
heavenly awareness). Pound's admired thinkers praise the seen
form, the manifest, the tangible real that must form the base for
meditation:

> The ragged arab spoke with Frobenius and told him
> The names of 3000 plants.
>   Bruhl found some languages full of detail
> Words that half mimic action; but
> generalization is beyond them, a white dog is
> not, let us say, a dog like a black dog.
>
>   [38/189:197]

One must start from a real not an abstract place. It is in this
context or position that one must understand the provocative
line, "sacrum, sacrum, illuminatio coitu" ("sacred, sacred, the
knowledge of [from] coitus"). The line has been wrenched out
of context in some criticism to make Pound appear to have been
a voluptuary, or a devotee of Eleusian or Bacchic cultism or
mysticism, and then to interpret the crucial Cantos 39 and 47
from these perspectives. Such readings are, to me, warping and
simplistic. Pound, seen in the totality of *The Cantos,* is no more
a devotee of the Eleusian rites than he is of the rites of *Li-Ki* or
muan bpo (to be discussed later); rather he loves their effects on
the human sensibility. Cantos 39 and 47 are not about coition,
but about art. The sexual theme is there, but subordinate, and
reflects the same ambivalent attitudes towards the theme
expressed in Cantos 27 to 30.

> From star up to the half-dark
> From half-dark to half-dark
> >   Unceasing the measure
> Flank by flank on the headland
> >   with the Goddess' eyes to seaward
> By Circeo, by Terracina, with the stone eyes
> >   white toward the sea
> With one measure, unceasing:
> >   "Fac deum!" "Est factus."
> Ver novum!
> >   ver novum!
> Thus made the spring, . . .

> [39/195:203]

"Unceasing the measure" could well stand as the central insight
repeated throughout *The Cantos:* the lyric impulse ever and
unceasingly transforming the heavily dualistic experience of
reality into new psychic springtimes. Lovers by the sea "make
Gods" and goddesses, transform what can be the drugged glut of
sexual relations ("spring overborne into summer," Circe
transforming men into swine) into spiritual, creative freshness,
new lyric song. As Pound says later, "And who no longer make
gods out of beauty / this is a dying" (113/786:16). The landscape
of half-light on a headland to represent the lyric light in the
darkness of experience is reminiscent of the imagery in the early
poem, "The Coming of War: Actaeon":

> An image of Lethe,
> >   and the fields
> Full of faint light
> >   but golden,
> Gray cliffs,
> >   and beneath them
> A sea
> Harsher than granite,
> >   unstill, never ceasing;
> High forms
> >   with the movement of gods, . . .

Circeo and Terracina are geographical place names associated, respectively, with the Circe legend and with a temple to the goddess Aphrodite. The latter, Terracina, recurs throughout the later cantos (pp. 435:462, 754:779). The "stone eyes" of the white marble goddess suggests both the blankness of real stone and the vision, the light, that the eye of the believer or the perceiver can put there. The lovers "can see but their eyes in the dark . . . / Beaten from flesh into light" (39/195:204). What the poet sees, what remains from the anvil of time is a series of lyrical moments lifted out of the imperfections of real situations, sexual or otherwise. The scene in Circe's ingle (see *Odyssey*, Loeb ed., X:133ff.) with which the canto opens is but one among many examples in Canto 39 and throughout *The Cantos* of the transformation of the insufficiencies of the quotidian ("erebus," "hell") into the "Lady" (Circe, Aphrodite, or Hathor, Mava, Flora, the Virgin, the Handmaid, the Bride, all in Canto 39, or the pastoral maiden of Canto 29, or Leucothea of Canto 95). The songs under Circe's olive and later in the canto of the headland are "sharp," "sharp at the edge," distinguishing sharply, precisely, dualistic reality from lyric vision.

> The cut cool of the air,
> Blossom cut on the wind, by Helios
> Lord of the Light's edge, and April
> Blown round the feet of the God,
> Beauty on an ass-cart
> Sitting on five sacks of laundry
>
> [29/145:150]

> there in the glade
> To Flora's night, with hyacinthus,
> With the crocus (spring
>   sharp in the grass) . . .
>
> ERI MEN AI DE KUDONIAI [In the Spring the Quinces]
> Betuene Aprile and Merche
>   with sap new in the bough
> With plum flowers above them
>   with almond on the black bough
>
> [39/195:203]

The "April" motif, representing the lyric moment when the mind has its paradise and its god, links the ancient Greek poet Ibycus's line to the line from the medieval English ballad to Pound's line ("Blown round the feet of the God"). There are allusions, too, in Canto 39 to Virgil, Catullus, Ovid, the Egyptian myth of Hathor, the Old and New Testaments, the "Pervigilium Veneris," and to Dante, as well as to Homer and the Eleusian mysteries—in short, the canto is another lyric meditation on the lyric in history ("the flowering almond") that informs also the myriad detail of Canto 20. Lyric song is always of the poignant "sharp edge" of light with darkness, lust with love, tragic song ("*illa dolore*," p. 194:202) with ecstatic song ("*Ver novum!*"), of the dualism that is the experience of the mind. It is the mind in its springtime spirit ("Mava") that can release Hathor from her prison box on the waves (as Leucothea saves Ulysses in Canto 95). Circe represents, however, the beautiful sensual world unmastered by the creative mind (the mind drugged in a sty of sensuality). The sty of sensuality is preferable, no question, to Eurilochus' fate, who did not partake of the sensual world and ended up as Poseidon's victim at the bottom of the sea. But, preferable to both Eurilochus' condition and Ulysses' condition under Circe, is the psychic moment where the sensual life is transformed by the divine in man's mind. The imagery allegorizing this process, or this lyric or visionary moment, alludes to the Virgin birth in the New Testament, to various blessed births celebrated in Old Testament song, and to the numerous impregnations of the human with the divine in pagan mythology:

> Beaten from flesh into light
> Hath swallowed the fire-ball
> A traverso le foglie [through the leaves]
> His rod hath made god in my belly
>   Sic loquitur nupta [So the bride speaks]
>   Cantat sic nupta [So the bride sings]

Dark shoulders have stirred the lightning
A girl's arms have nested the fire,
Not I but the handmaid kindled
    Cantat sic nupta
I have eaten the flame.

                              [39/196:204]

Circe is the real; the "bride" nourishes the artistic transformation
of the real. It is the poet who answers the call "fac deum," who
"makes god," the creative flow kindled by Circe and what she
represents. The sun-god, the "flame," the light that filters
through the leaves, is received by the "bride," the eager mind of
the poet, the intelligence that can perceive it, and conceive.[2]

    Canto 47 is like Canto 39, a meditation on the creative
mind, the light within reality, and uses, too, in places, figurations
from the sexual life:

The light has entered the cave. Io! Io!
The light has gone down into the cave,
Splendour on splendour!
By prong have I entered these hills:
That the grass grow from my body,
That I hear the roots speaking together,
The air is new on my leaf,
The forked boughs shake with the wind.
Is Zephyrus more light on the bough, Apeliota
More light on the almond branch?
By this door have I entered the hill.

                              [47/238:248]

The "official" commentary on these lines, as well as the whole
of Canto 47, ought to be compiled primarily from the close
analysis of the lyric passages of Cantos 16–30 (not, I should add,
from, say, Gourmont and Frazer, as has been the case), as Canto
47 recapitulates the imagery and attitudes developed in those
cantos. The passage above is not of the illuminations of coitus,
though that illumination was not, is not, to be denied:

> To the cave art thou called, Odysseus,
> By Molü has thou respite for a little,
> By Molü art thou freed from the one bed
>   that thou may'st return to another . . .
> By this gate art thou measured
> Thy day is between a door and a door . . .
> Yet hast thou gnawed through the mountain, . . .
> Hast thou entered more deeply the mountain?

[47/237:247]

To enter more deeply the mountain is allegorically to have sailed beyond the insufficiencies of the quotidian ("out of which things seeking an exit," Canto 40) and of the sexual life (albeit temporarily), and reach once more "that place."

> and I through this, and into the earth,
>   patet terra [the earth lies open]
> entered the quiet air
>   the new sky,
> the light as after a sun-set, . . .

[16/69:73]

It is to have gone through "door" or "gate" (see Canto 15/66–67:70–71) into "hill" or "mountain" (see Cantos 16/68–69:72–73; 17/76–77:80–81; 20/94–95:98–99; and passim in *The Pisan Cantos*) or "cave" (see Canto 17/76–77: 80–81; and passim in in Cantos 90–95) via the creative imagination, figured as "Molü," gift of the gods (see *Odyssey*, Loeb ed., X:286–306): "that hath the gift of healing, / that hath the power over wild beasts" (47/239:249), which gift Ulysses has, as does Bacchus (Canto 2), as does the poet who transforms "jungle" beasts into "ferae familiares" (see Canto 20/94:98, and later 76/457:486). For the "splendor" of the passage in Canto 47 see the "splendor of that day" in Canto 17/79:83, and compare the "vines bursting" from the poet's fingers there (17/76:80) with the "grass" growing from his body here, the "new air" here with the "new sky" of Canto 16/69:73, the almond branches here with the almond branches of Cantos 17/77:81 and 20/89–90:93–94.

The moment in "that place" comes and goes, one enters the door, gate, cave, or mountain, and then one must leave and go back into time, there where social (and sexual) rituals are for good or not so good (for good, see the passage from Hesiod's *Work and Days,* or that from the *Li Ki* in Canto 52), but never so good as the dimension of stillness, outside of time, of the visionary moment or mood. To enter the mountain, where one desires to be, by "gnawing" or by "prong" (cf. by "rod" of Canto 39) carries an ironic, albeit sexual, tone of the serio-comic. Purposely, the words are not decorous in the lyric context; one is not entering the mountain, as is the representative of the baroque vision at the end of Canto 20, in a carriage on the high road. The poet of the twentieth century is measured by the lyricism he can maintain in a world depopulated by gods: "Knowledge the shade of a shade, / Yet must thou sail after knowledge / Knowing less than drugged beasts" (47/236:246). Thus it is that the modern poet sets up "little lights in a great darkness" (as did ancient peoples literally in fertility rituals):

> The small lamps drift in the bay
> And the sea's claw gathers them . . .
> The white teeth gnaw in under the crag,
> But in the pale night the small lamps float seaward
>
> [p. 236:246]

We have met the motif earlier:

> Dye-pots in the torch-light
> The flash of wave under prows, . . .
>
> [17/78:82]

> And in the barche with lanthorns;
> The prows rose silver on silver
>   taking light in the darkness.
>
> [26/121:126]

> Silver beaks out of night, . . .
>   lamps fluid in water,
>
> [29/146:151]

And we will meet it again, in Canto 49/244:255, and in Canto 90 (p. 607:641), and 91 (p. 612:646). The ocean of "teeth" and "claw" of Canto 47 casts an even longer dualistic shadow than the reiterated "darkness" of earlier lyric passages. Hardly the atmospheric setting for a simply ecstatic, Bacchic ritual of Eleusis; the tone is rather that of Bion's elegiac "Lament For Adonis," from which comes the canto's chant: "TU DIONA / *Kai* MOIRAI' ADONIN" [You Diona (Aphrodite) and the / Fates (cry over) Adonis] (47/236:246). Adonis in the old rituals comes again in a "new spring": "Wheat shoots rise new by the altar, / flower from the swift seed" (p. 237:247). In the rituals of art, as Pound has been saying over and over again, one worships the "new stone" (cf. "The stone is alive in my hand," Canto 6/21:25), new sculpture, new forms by artists who do not survive their accomplishments.[3]

> Forked shadow falls dark on the terrace
> More black than the floating martin
> > that has no care for your presence,
> His wing-print is black on the roof tiles
> And the print is gone with his cry.
> So light is thy weight on Tellus
> Thy notch no deeper indented
> Thy weight less than the shadow
> Yet has thou gnawed through the mountain,
> > Scylla's white teeth less sharp.

[p. 237:248]

There is no better passage to illustrate Pound's absolute integrity of vision in his lyric modes—the artist and his work as of very little consequence and as of very great and triumphant consequence. The recurring motif (Cantos 36/177:182; 79/492:525; 80/515:550) of no "weight" perfectly serves the ambivalent tone desired, as it can suggest both transcendent vision and wholly subjective vision. The poet, like Ulysses (cf. *Odyssey*, Loeb ed., X:490-95) must "go the road to hell," that is, experience, which includes adventure and blind death (as

Adonis'), Circe and plowing, disorder and ritual, darkness and vision—no escape from the process, but the chance for achievement ("fertility") within it:

> By this gate art thou measured . . .
> Hast'ou a deeper planting, doth thy death year
> Bring swifter shoot?
> Hast thou entered more deeply the mountain?
>
> [47/237:247]

Pound always has in *The Cantos* two answers to the hell of experience: one, the "dimension of stillness" "outside" of time, the visionary moment or lyric meditation, the other, the participation in the world of action by the "doers," the "men of craft," *adepti,* men who have had or have a vision of a "Lady," of a "City," of a good society; men such as Emperor Tsing of Canto 49. It is the effect of Canto 49 to dramatize the psychological tranquility, not of a man of action, but of an anonymous Chinese peasant who looks out onto a landscape heavily colored in his own subjective awareness by coldness and darkness, rain and weeping, sparseness and emptiness, and yet who has the keenness of perception and delicacy of response to love what light or beauty comes to his place.

> Under the cabin roof was one lantern.
> The reeds are heavy; bent;
> and the bamboos speak as if weeping . . .
> Sail passed here in April; may return in October
> Boat fades in silver; slowly;
> Sun blaze alone on the river . . .
>
> Comes then snow scur on the river
> And a world is covered with jade
> Small boat floats like a lanthorn,
> The flowing water clots as with cold . . .
> Rooks clatter over the fishermen's lanthorns,
> A light moves on the north sky line
>
> [49/244:255]

The motif of small boats and lanthorns, the boats in a silver landscape, keeps recurring to enforce the effect of the central metaphor, "In the gloom, the gold / Gathers the light about it" (Canto 17/78:82); the "world covered with jade" and the "sun-blaze" represent such a process of gathering of precious moments of perception and response typical, it seems, of Chinese poetry and painting. Such tranquility of spirit comes not only from the acceptance of dualistic process but also from being far from the corruptions of riches and imperial power. The two ancient lyrics with which the canto ends speak of this spirit and of its reward, delicacy of perception. Such a spirit is but one avenue, one road to the "dimension of stillness" with which the lyric passages of *The Cantos* are always concerned. The key iterative phrase for the power of that "moment," that "place," "the power over wild beasts," is here at the end of Canto 49 as it was at the end of Canto 47, but more poignant, for the peasant's condition seems so very powerless, his sensitive spirit transforming into beauty what can appear to the vulgar (the "wild beasts," especially the usurious and the power-hungry) a cold and hard existence.[4]

It is the creative imagination in its moments that is called the "mind of heaven":

> Shines
> in the mind of heaven God
> who made it
> more than the sun
> in our eye.

[51/250:261]

Our minds illumine or transform nature, since the mind's light is "more than the sun." The idea is pervasive in *The Cantos* from Canto 17, "The light now, not of the sun" in the cave of Nerea (17/76:80) to Canto 106, "the light blazed behind her/nor was this from sunset" (106/754:779) referring to the stone eyes of the marble Aphrodite. All we can do is worship the light of the

mind as a product of "God," the "NOUS," "ineffable crystal."
Pound's "God" represents the tranquility, repose of spirit, to
which we can only aspire.

> Out of which things seeking an exit
> To the high air, to the stratosphere, to the imperial
> calm, to the empyrean, to the baily of the four towers
> the NOUS, the ineffable crystal . . .
>
> [40/201:209]

Hanno in his "periplum" (as we in ours) can hope, therefore,
only for better earthly empires (as Napoleon's vision in Canto
44, or Pietro Leopold's in Canto 42) and better cities (as he who
sees "cities move in one figure" in Canto 42/213:221, as Pound
in *The Pisan Cantos,* or as those "founders, gazing at the mounts
of their cities" of Canto 15/69:73); he cannot hope for, say, the
"empyrean," Dante's Tenth Heaven, or for any other
transcendent heaven. Our paradises are painted or incised on
church walls (Canto 45) only and represent "plies" or "layers"
of consciousness or illumination (better or lesser crystal gems):
adept fly-fishing, for instance, (Canto 51/251:262) one layer,
seeing the true effects of usury (though not knowing how to
cope with it) another: "and the light became so bright and so
blindin' / in this layer of paradise / that the mind of man was
bewildered" (38/190:198). One ply or layer of the mind of
heaven is simple and of the peasantry—all the villagers going out
to build the cathedral (27/130:135) or to celebrate the priest's
first mass (48/242:252), or the Sienese women in the oxen
procession (43/216:225), or the Chinese women offering
cocoons to the "Son of Heaven" in the *Li Ki* (52/258:269), the
Greek woman doing the same for Thamuz (91/612:646). Other
layers of the mind of heaven, of created earthly paradises in the
mind or a society, are of the order of complexity of the arts and
sciences (the analogy in the layers motif to Dante's ascent in the
Paradiso through the ten heavens is obvious; Pound's use of
Dantean paradigms is, of course, pervasive in *The Cantos*):

That hath the light of the doer, as it were
a form cleaving to it.
Deo similis quodam modo
hic intellectus adeptus

[51/251:262]

The Latin ("Godlike in a way / This intellect that has grasped")
is from Albertus Magnus (see Pound's *Literary Essays,* p. 186);
in Pound's context it asserts that the spirit that loves to do
something well (be it fly-fishing, sculpture, or canal building) is
blessed in comparison to those who may have money or power
or hold to one fanaticism or other, but have no light, no sense
of order or form (*Ching ming,* or *To Kalon*) within themselves
or their works.

The lengthy passage from the ancient Chinese text, the *Li
Ki* (Book of Rites), is but one such making of social order (as
Hesiod's *Works and Days* of Canto 47 and the *muan bpo* of the
late cantos) out of disorder, dicta which may or may not have
any metaphysical foundation but encompass close observation
and lovely ritual:

    Month of the longest days
Life and death are now equal
        Strife is between light and darkness
Wise man stays in his house . . .
Offer to gods of the hearth
        the lungs of the victims
Warm wind is rising, cricket bideth in wall
Young goshawk is learning his labour
        dead grass breedeth glow-worms.

[52/259:269]

The Chinese vision at its best, the Confucian (as in Canto
13), as it filters through Pound, accepts the dualistic condition
of man ("some things cannot be changed," 54/275:286), traces
the wisest course within it (the "Process"), and despises
metaphysical pontificating and dogmatism. Cantos 53–61 are
dominated by this vision, as are *The Cantos* as a whole, for it is
Pound's vision:

sieges from the beginning of time until now.
sieges, court treasons and laziness,
Against order, lao, bhud and lamas,
      night clubs, empresses' relatives, and hoang miao,
            [Foreigners]
poisoning life with mirages, ruining order; TO KALON
         [The Beautiful]
              [58/318:332]

The beautiful in Chinese culture we can sense in Pound's
Cathay, his *Confucius,* and his *The Book of Odes,* in the respect
there for the arts and letters and for good conversation and lyric
song. "Foreigners," of course, have their own beautiful orders,
which just as invariably rise and fall. Witness the destruction at
Mt. Segur in Provence:

Falling Mars in the air . . .

where was spire-top a-level the grass yard
Then the towers, high over chateau—
Fell with stroke after stroke . . .
              [48/243:253]

    Hence the form of the Chinese cantos that seem to many
readers endless, pointless repetition: the psychological
establishment of the tragic, cyclic view of history via the
incantatory (and quite easy to read) overview of 4,000 years of
Chinese history. And hence the importance of the early
emperor's injunction to "make it new," for all beauty or order
will fall and must be established again in a new context.
    Hence, too, the idea that seems so incongruous to many
readers as it runs throughout *The Cantos:* the importance of
law and constitutions and of precise definition and strict
construction thereof. A functioning order productive of some
beauty and equity and grace of social living (e.g., fascists="rods
in a bundle," Canto 52/272:282) ought not to be tampered
with much or subjected to much foreign influence that,
however good in its own context, is without root in the new soil.

Forms often outlive their contexts (though sometimes, as with
Confucianism in China, rise again):

> And as after the form, the shadow,
> Noble forms, lacking life . . .
> the dead words keeping form
> and the cry: Civis Romanus
>
> [25/118:123]

Constitutions and precisely formulated laws that follow the first
principles of the constitution provide for the possibility of
continuity of a given society, for order, ritual, beauty, to
flourish and continue to flourish. This, in Pound's view, was
John Adams's basic insight in his journals:

> . . . and mankind dare not yet think upon
>   CONSTITUTIONS . . .
>
> [68/395:416]

> the people are addicted, as well as the great,
>   to corruption . . .
>
> [62/345:361]

>   whenever
> we leave principles and clear propositions
> and wander into construction we wander into a wilderness . . . ,
>
> [64/358:376]

> foundation of every government in some principle
> or passion of the people
>   *ma che si sente dicho* . . .
>   ["is felt, I say"–Cavalcanti]
> empire of laws not of men . . .
>
> [67/391:411]

> MISERIA servitus, ubi jus vagum
> [service is a misery when rights are vague]
>
> [68/396:417]

These were the insights, too, of Pound's later cultural hero
Edmund Coke (whom Adams too admired, Canto 62/343:359).
Adams and Eleusis, Coke and *Li Ki,* Mussolini and *To*

Kalon, curious combinations until one sees that what is important for Pound is the creation of social contexts where from some beauty, be it arts or letters, lyric song or lovely ritual, an ethical or scientific or craft standard, has flowed or might flow. The Cavalcanti quotation in the Adams passage (and there are other such interpolated in the Adams cantos) is not intended to demonstrate that there is one metaphysic linking Adams to Cavalcanti or, say, Grosseteste to Cleanthes, or Provence to China; the link in the passage concerns "passion" and "feeling": what is felt deeply, finely, and with some community, is what inspires "love" in a people and, ultimately, beautiful forms in an ordered society. There *are,* to be sure, intellectual relationships between, say, Cleanthes' sense of natural law (71/421:443; translation on p. 256:446) and Confucius's sense of the unwobbling pivot or the process, but the relation is abstract and not as important to Pound as the effects of the sanctification of life apparent in an Aphrodite cult at Terracina or the bringing of grain to the *Manes* of Mt. Taishan.[5] Pound's life is wrecked between the period of these cantos of the thirties and those to come, but these central ideas are embodied in *The Pisan Cantos* and the later cantos in their lyric and nonlyric modalities.

5: THE PISAN CANTOS

The *Pisan Cantos*, so called because "they were composed when the poet was incarcerated in a prison camp near Pisa" from May to December 1945, were published by New Directions in July 1948. They read as extended meditation of a poet who, in tragic circumstances, reviews his life, his major ideas, and loves ("How is it far, if you think of it?" p. 465:495). If my articulation of the poet's most deeply felt attitudes in the lyric passages of *The Cantos* until this point has useful validity, the major positions and imagistic motifs of *The Pisan Cantos* ought to be illuminated by the earlier analyses. There are, in *The Pisan Cantos*, few "set" lyrical passages alternating with set narrative or discursive passages, as in the earlier cantos. The meditating mind jumps from discursive statement to lyric statement as the will dictates,

and it is for the reader to grasp the thematic or imagistic or
emotional associations that link the collages of elliptical phrases
and passages that constitute the new technical triumph of *The
Pisan Cantos*. I do not feel that these linkages or the passages
themselves are claustrophobically private, as hostile criticism
would have it. I will note where certain motifs in the lyrical
passages of *The Pisan Cantos* (and the later cantos) escape my
analysis, but in each instance I have the feeling that the gap will
be filled by next year's scholar. The fragmented, elliptical style
of these later cantos makes it impossible to point out each lyric
or mythological or visionary phrase that appears, but I have
made every attempt to clarify all the major lyric "nodes" or
"clusters," and to avoid none.

   The Pisan Cantos alternate moments of close analysis of
the poet's present situation, observation of his surroundings, the
prison camp life, the clouds above, the earth beneath, with
moments of despair ("hell," "erebus," "phlegethon," "lethe,"
"shipwreck," "seadrift," and "seepage") and with the
contrasting moments of lyric exultation, the intermittent,
subjective, psychic elevation to "that place" of stillness and
serenity about which Pound has written variations so often in
the earlier cantos:

> Lay in soft grass by the cliff's edge
>   with the sea 30 metres below this
>   and at hand's span, at cubit's reach moving,
> the crystalline, as inverse of water,
>   clear over rock-bed
>
>   ac ferae familiares [and tame animals]
> the gemmed field *a destra* with fawn, with panther,
>   corn flower, thistle and sword-flower
>   to a half metre grass growth,
> lay on the cliff's edge
>   . . . nor is this yet *atasal*
>   nor are here souls, nec personae
>   neither here in hypostasis, this land is of Dione

and under her planet
    to Helia the long meadow with poplars
to   Κύπρις [Cypris, Aphrodite]
    the mountain and shut garden of pear trees in flower
here rested.

                            [77/457:486]

The crystalline vision is in the mind ("at hand's span," cf. 15/66:70, "half the width of a sword's edge"), and is the inverse of sea water that is without form or light or stability. In the vision are the tame animals of Cantos 2, 17, 20, 39, 47, and 49. This place is of "Dione," "Helia," "Aphrodite," what goddess you will, for it is of the divine light in man's mind. Pear trees are here rather than the almond trees of Cantos 17, 20, 39, and 47, rather than the pomegranate trees of Canto 79. It does not matter, for the vision is not an absolute but a series of poetic images to describe a "state of mind," "hypostasis," not "atasal." The latter terms are from medieval philosophy, "hypostasis" signifying the manifestly real from which metaphysics begins, "atasal" the spirit's "union with god" which metaphysics desires. Pound's own gloss is "spiriti questi? personae? [are these spirits? persons?] / tangibility by no means *atasal*" (77/459:487). The figures of Aphrodite and of panthers (lynxes later) are not metaphysical absolutes, whatever the ontological status of the grass, cornflower, thistle (and later, morning-glory and clover, ant, spider, lizard, wasp, and butterfly), the manifest. There is no problem, for the mind loves the vision whatever its status: "there came new subtlety of eyes into my tent, / whether of spirit or hypostasis . . ." (81/520:555).

It may be that the "drama is wholly subjective" (74/430:457): "bricks thought into being ex nihil / suave in the cavity of the rock la concha" (76/462:491). This last line is a reminiscence of Canto 17 and the "Cave of Nerea," "she like a great shell curved / In the suavity of the rock" (17/76:80). The cave, there and elsewhere, represents the mind creating its own place, its earthly paradises, temples, and cities. "Bricks thought into being ex nihil" is but a more direct statement of what has been said in *The Cantos* from the beginning: that the mind will not tolerate emptiness, meaninglessness, in its ambience:

> How soft the wind under Taishan
> > where the sea is remembered
> out of hell, the pit
> out of the dust and glare evil
> Zephyrus / Apeliota
> This liquid is certainly a
> > property of the mind
> nec accidens est but an element
> > in the mind's make-up
> est agens and functions dust to a fountain pan otherwise
> Hast'ou seen the rose in the steel dust . . .?
>
> > > [74/449:477]

"Taishan"—literally, a holy mountain with temples, in China—is in *The Pisan Cantos* any mountain; it is "Taishan @ Pisa" (p. 427:453), it is "Taishan-Chocorua" (p. 530:565, with reference to Vermont's Mt. Chocorua). The wind has any name: "Zephyrus," "Apeliota" (see 47/238:248), "Kuanon," because it is the mind that creates the soft, liquid "wind," the "spiritus," not reality, where "no wind is the king's wind" (4/16:20). Reality is often hell ("out of erebus," "phlegethon"), the pit, the dust. It is the mind that is the force, the will, the agent, that orders, as a magnet orders, steel dust into a rose pattern.

It is the mind which nourishes dreams of new cities, new societies, out of its own "liquid":

> Δρυάς, your eyes are like the clouds over Taishan
> > When some of the rain has fallen
> > and half remains yet to fall
>
> The roots go down to the river's edge
> > and the hidden city moves upward
> > white ivory under the bark
>
> With clouds over Taishan-Chocorua . . .
> Plura diafana [many diaphans]

> Heliads lift the mist from the young willows
> there is no base seen under Taishan
>   but the brightness of *'udor* [water]
> The poplar tips float in brightness . . .
>
> [83/530:565]

There is no base to the mountain or to the city in ivory or to the trees. We have seen the images of floating forests and columns of stone or marble in Cantos 17 and 29, and the "wood/white under new cortex" in Canto 25 (p. 117:122), all representing the "ex nihil" creative power of the human imagination. The light of the mind ("not of the sun," p. 76:80) is the brightness that lifts the "mist" or "cloud," not all the way, but enough to bring the human spirit out of darkness, out of hell. The mind cannot reach *atasal* but must remain in the phenomenological realm of "plura diaphana," of dancing "graces" or "heliads," of the dryad's eyes or of Aphrodite's.

All of which leads us back to the beginning of *The Pisan Cantos:*

> To build the city of Dioce whose terraces are the colour
>   of stars.
> The suave eyes, quiet, not scornful,
>   rain also is of the process . . .
> "the great periplum brings in the stars to our shore."
> You who have passed the pillars and outward from Herakles
> when Lucifer fell in N. Carolina.
> if the suave air give way to scirocco
>   ΟΎ ΤΙΣ, ΟΎ ΤΙΣ ? Odysseus
>   the name of my family.
> the wind also is of the process,
>   sorella la luna
>
> [74/425:451]

The collage of images represents the full awareness in the prisoner/poet of the dualistic nature of the "process" or "natural law," as defined by Confucius in his "Unwobbling Pivot." The passage (as the whole of *The Pisan Cantos*) is both

autobiographical and representative of the condition in which
every adventurer of the spirit (every "Odysseus") will at some
time find himself; the time of rain and evil wind ("scirocco")
must be accepted, just as blessed moments of light and vision
("suave air," "Kuanon," "Zephyr") are praised ("Introibo," p.
513:548, "m'elevasti," p. 606:640). The "city of Dioce" is
representative of any new "building" based on a coherent and
humane vision, be it a society or a poem (for "Dioce"
specifically see Herodotus, Loeb ed., 1:98 on "Ecbatana," and
also The Cantos, pp. 16–17:20–21).[1] To partially realize one's
vision in the world of circumstances is to be partially blessed by
the goddess's (here, Aphrodite's) glance ("quiet not scornful,"
cf. "saw but the eyes," p. 520:556). It is the sun (Helios) that
sails or wheels about the universe daily on his "great periplum"
leading his "fleet" of clouds (p. 452:480). The sun's daily voyage
perhaps inspired early religious myth and the Ulysses myth
(among others), just as the rising and falling of the morning star
("Lucifer") may have inspired the myth of the fallen angel
("North Carolina" representing the "West" to the Mediterranean
observer). All poets generally can be seen as $O\dot{Y}\ TI\Sigma$, no man,
insignificant; Pound, in particular, in his straits, could be seen as
a fallen, broken man. But just as Ulysses used the "no man"
phrase in an immortal poem, just as Elpenor requested of
Ulysses the prophetic epitaph "a man of no fortune and with a
name to come" (pp. 4:8, 439:466), so does the lyric poet,
generally, and Pound, specifically, hope that the cunning hand
at the lyric may give the poet immortality. The poet speaks to
the sun ("you who have passed the pillars") in a brotherly way,
just as St. Francis speaks to the moon as his sister ("sorella") in
his "Cantico del Sole." Sun and moon together preside as
natural dieties in The Pisan Cantos, "femina, femina . . ./
under the gray cliff in periplum / the sun dragging her stars"
(74/431:457). It is this effect of the poetic consciousness, this
mythologizing of nature, sun, moon, hills, and streams, that
humanizes the universe and makes it comprehensible.

It is not metaphysics that makes his life a blessing when it is a blessing, not the dogma nor the sophistication of the reasoning, but the affection that mythology or poetry can produce in the mind's ambience. Thus it is that Pound can equate the vision of a St. Francis or a Confucius with that of an anonymous Sudanese folk tale, "and with one day's reading a man may have the key in / his hands / Lute of Gassir. Hooo Fasa" (74/427:454). Once one looks closely at the legend in the version Pound used (Frobenius and Fox, *African Genesis* [New York: Stackpole Sons, 1937], pp. 97–110), it becomes clear just how striking a parallel the allegorical import of its motifs makes to the body of attitudes implicit in *The Cantos*. The tale is of the "city" of "Wagadu":

> Four times Wagadu stood there in all her splendor. Four times Wagadu disappeared and was lost to human sight: once through vanity, once through falsehood, once through greed and once through dissension. Four times Wagadu changed her name. First she was called Dierra, then Agada, then Ganna, then Silla. Four times she turned her face. Once to the north, once to the west, once to the east and once to the south. For Wagadu, whenever men have seen her, has always had four gates, one to the north, one to the west, one to the east and one to the south. Those are the directions whence the strength of Wagadu comes, the strength in which she endures no matter whether she be built of stone, wood and earth or lives but as a shadow in the mind and longing of her children. For really, Wagadu is not of stone, not of wood, not of earth. Wagadu is the strength which lives in the hearts of men and is sometimes visible because eyes see her and ears hear the clash of swords and ring of shields, and is sometimes invisible because the indomitability of men has overtired her, so that she sleeps. Sleep came to Wagadu for the first time through vanity, for the second time through falsehood, for the third time through greed and for the fourth time through dissension. Should Wagadu ever be found for the fourth time, then she will live so forcefully in the minds of men that she will never be lost again, so forcefully that vanity, falsehood, greed and dissension will never be able to harm her.

Hoooh! Dierra, Agada, Ganna, Silla! Hoooh! Fasa!
[Frobenius, pp. 97-98]

Whatever the specific significance to the Fasa tribe, the image of
the city of Wagadu as the strength that lives in the hearts of
men, and is visible only to some men at some times, clearly· can
serve the lyric poet as an intuitive representation of the poetic
consciousness of any time or nation (four gates of entry, north,
west, east, and south). The parallel of the poetic consciousness
in the image of a divine female awaking to the image of
Aphrodite's stone eyes again turning seaward (the "voyager's"
prayer) recurrent in *The Cantos* is also striking:

As by Terracina rose from the sea Zephyr behind her . . .
    till the shrine be again white with marble
    till the stone eyes look again seaward
[74/435:461]

These parallels must have seemed uncanny to Pound, but
perhaps more so the legend's own subsequent direct linkage of
the "strength of man" to the poetic consciousness:

One night Gassire sprang out of bed, left the
house and went to an old wise man, a man who knew more
than other people. He entered the wise man's house and asked:
"Kiekorro! When will my father, Nganamba, die and leave me
his sword and shield?" The old man said: "Ah, Gassire,
Nganamba will die; but he will not leave you his sword and
shield! You will carry a lute. Shield and sword shall others
inherit . . . .
                        your path will lead you to
the partridges in the fields and you will understand what they
say and that will be your say and the way of Wagadu.
[Frobenius, p. 100]

which path followed leads to a surprising dualistic song of the
process:

> The partridge sang: All
> creatures must die, be buried and rot, Kings and heroes die, are
> buried and rot, I, too, shall die, shall be buried and rot. But the
> *Dausi,* the song of my battles, shall not die. It shall be sung
> again and again and shall outlive all kings and heroes. Hoooh.
> that I might do such deeds! Hoooh, that I may sing the *Dausi!*
> Wagadu will be lost. But the *Dausi* shall endure and shall live!
> [Frobenius, p. 101]

The position is, I think, quintessential Pound, "Wagadu" will be lost, forty times four times, but the dreams of Wagadu, never: "I believe in the resurrection of Italy, quia impossibile est / 4 times to the song of Gassire / now in the mind indestructible" (74/442:470). Gassire's song to be immortal must be of the dualism:

> The smith said: "This is a piece of wood. It cannot sing if it
> has no heart. You must give it a heart. Carry this piece of
> wood on your back when you go into battle. The wood must
> ring with the stroke of your sword. The wood must absorb
> down dripping blood, blood of your blood, breath of your
> breath. Your pain must be its pain, your fame its fame. The
> wood may no longer be like the wood of a tree, but must be
> penetrated by and be a part of your people. Therefore it must
> live not only with you but with your sons. Then will the tone
> that comes from your heart echo in the ear of your son and
> live on in the people, and your son's life's blood, oozing out of
> his heart, will run down your body and live on in this piece of
> wood. (Frobenius, p. 103)

All of which comes to pass after Gassire loses seven sons and his father. What is stressed in the legend of Gassire's lute, and what I think needs to be stressed in Pound's *Cantos,* is the recognition as part of the process of both the destructiveness of history and the concomitant importance of the poetic consciousness building myth, ritual, and art.

"Aram vult nemus"—"the grove needs an altar"—echoes

throughout *The Pisan Cantos* (pp. 446:473, 481:512, 492:525),
as does later "The Temple is not for sale" (pp. 676–79, 707–11,
721:749), both of which are variations, for a poet of Pound's
way of seeing, of "I don't know how humanity stands it / with a
painted paradise at the end of it / without a painted paradise at
the end of it" (74/436:463), for the religious impulse (hunger
for paradise after death) and the aesthetic impulse (paradise
painted on a church wall, cf. 45/229:239) both satisfy the need
of the human spirit for meaning. When one is down, or when
one is permanently or temporarily a skeptical "Tovarisch" (pp.
131:136, 430:456), art can seem meaningless: "Teofile's
bricabrac Cocteau's bricabrac / sea drift snowin' 'em under /
every man to his junk-shop" (76/453:481). But Pound is never
down very long. The last line of this passage is, in fact, but an
ironic allusion to the echoing line in *The Pisan Cantos* (pp.
435:461, 443:471, 454:482, 479:510, 487:519, 540:575),
taken from *Micah* 4:5, concerning the power of the religious
impulse: "each one in his god's name."

The language and substance of legend, myth, religion, and
art are consistently and purposely fused in *The Pisan Cantos*
(and elsewhere):

> in principio verbum
> paraclete or the verbum perfectum: sinceritas
> from the death cells in sight of Mt. Taishan @ Pisa . . .
>
> [74/427:453]

> from Mt. Taishan to the sunset
> From Carrara stone to the tower
> and this day the air was made open
> for Kuanon of all delights,
> Linus, Cletus, Clement
> whose prayers,
> the great scarab is bowed at the altar
> the green light gleams in his shell
> plowed in the sacred field and unwound the silk worms early . . .
>
> [p. 428:455]

the paraclete that was present in Yao, the precision
in Shun the compassionate
in Yu the guider of waters . . .
Light tensile immaculata . . .

[p. 429:455]

and the nymph of the Hagoromo came to me
                    as a corona of angels
one day were clouds banked on Taishan
        or in glory of sunset . . .

[p. 430:456]

"Sinceritas" as defined in Pound's *Confucius* is "the precise
definition of the word, pictorially the sun's lance coming to rest
on the precise spot verbally." This ought to be the exalted aim
of the language of poetry and theology as well as of law and or
constitutions, the intelligence striving for precision concerning
contexts of feeling. The famous marble of Italian cities and
sculpture, of statues of Aphrodite early and of the Virgin later,
came from a quarry in Carrara, close to Pisa. "Kuanon" is the
oriental counterpart, the goddess of mercy, representing, in *The
Pisan Cantos,* no literal belief, but rather the sweet ligurian
breeze, and at the same time, the "spiritus" in man which
elevates the mind in its moments. Literal belief is likewise beside
the point in Pound's invocations of saints and spirits in all such
passages. "Linus, Cletus, Clement," all prayed to the Christian
God and had their moments; the ancient Egyptians prayed to
the scarab (cf. 3/11:15); the ancient Chinese women brought
cocoons to the Son of Heaven (cf. 52/258:269). The "paraclete"
refers not only to the Christian Holy Spirit, but to anyone called
to aid another, as, say, the mythical fathers of China, Yao, Shun,
and Yu (cf. 53/262-64:272-74). "Immaculata" is an epithet
for the Virgin Mary but serves as well for the crystal purity and
clarity of a poetic consciousness ("light") creating myths from a
precise understanding of what the heart desires (therefore an
"ex nihilo" and "immaculate" conception). The nymph ("moon
nymph immacolata," p. 500:534) of the oriental Noh play

Hagoromo coming to the poet surrounded by angels, as the
Virgin does in so many Renaissance Italian paintings, is an image
not without a certain self-irony, as is true in many of these
references, but dominant is the impulse toward "sinceritas"
with which the "mantle" of the poetic consciousness invests the
mind: "With us there is no deceit / said the moon nymph
immacolata / Give back my cloak, *hagoromo*." (80/500:534). It
is to that consciousness, not to the Virgin, that the poet prays
for intercession from spiritual drowning:

> Immaculata, Introibo
> > for those who drink of the bitterness
> Perpetua, Agatha, Anastasia
> > > saeculorum
>
> repos donnez à cils
> > senza termine funge Immaculata Regina
> > > Les larmes qui j'ai creées m'inondent
> Tard, très tard je t'ai connue, la Tristesse, . . .

[80/513:548]

The "Immaculata Regina" motif is picked up again in Canto 91
(p. 610:644), and there as here, it is a variation on the
omnipresent figure of the "Lady," representing the poetic
consciousness. The phrases from the Catholic mass and the
prayer to the Catholic female martyrs are, as in the passage
preceding, meant only to pay homage to the will to believe that
creates myths that in turn impel right action and good values.
Pound, like Villon, has lived a life of action and of meditation,
and is now almost broken by suffering and the impending death
that he may have brought upon himself, as he sees it, by his
"sinceritas" and his subsequent actions. He is left with solitude,
which is often terrible, sometimes lovely: "between NEKUIA
where are Alcmene and Tyro / and the Charybdis of action / to
the solitude of Mt. Taishan" (74/431:457). The "solitude" of
Mt. Taishan refers here to the blessed lyric or visionary mood
that can come to the meditations of the ascetic or to the

prisoner-poet, to the full range of the "paradisical" state of
mind (that solitude alternating with the solitude that is a
"hell"):

Le Paradis n'est pas artificiel

    but spezzato apparently
      it exists only in fragments unexpected excellent sausage,
          the smell of mint, for example,
        Ladro the night cat;
      at Nemi waited on the slope above the lake sunken in the
                        pocket of hills
      awaiting decision from the old lunch cabin built out
                    over the shingle,
    Zarathustra, now desuete
  to Jupiter and to Hermes where now is the castellaro
      no vestige save in the air

[74/438:465]

    Le Paradis n'est pas artificiel
        States of mind are inexplicable to us . . .
    Le paradis n'est pas artificiel,
        l'enfer non plus.

[76/460:488]

Here again the complex tonality typical of Pound, really of any
serious artist who is praising gods he does not literally believe in
("a god is an eternal state of mind"–"Religio," *Pavannes and
Divagations,* 1918). Life is good, Pound is saying, when people
believing in gods sacramentalize the hills (for the ritualists at
Nemi see Frazer's *Golden Bough*) with temples ("plural" Pound
emphasizes on p. 434:461); life is not good when the temples
and their devotions are replaced by castles or shacks. Such a
subjective "religious" position is difficult to maintain, hence the
humorous self-irony of the sausage fragment to represent the
blessedness of the lyric moment or state of mind. The position
is repeated not in an ironic but in a tragic context in Canto 92:
"Le Paradis n'est pas artificiel / but is jagged, / For a flash, / for
an hour. / Then agony, / then an hour, / then agony

[92/620:653]. This alternation of attitude cannot be resolved; it is the dilemma of a felt dualism that Pound faces and dramatizes.

There is a strong undercurrent of irony in the celebrated lyric to the "lynx," the guardian of "goddesses" and "gardens," that is, of the lyric mood:

> O Lynx, my love, my lovely lynx,
> Keep watch over my wine pot,
> Guard close my mountain still
> Till the god come into this whiskey
> Manitou, god of lynxes, remember our corn.
> Khardas, god of camels
>   what the deuce are you doing here?
>
> [79/487:520]

> Maelid and bassarid among lynxes;
>   how many? There are more under the oak trees,
> We are here waiting the sun-rise
>   and the next sunrise
> for three nights amid lynxes. For three nights
>   of the oak-wood
> and the vines are thick in their branches
>   no vine lacking flower,
> no lynx lacking a flower rope
>   no Maelid minus a wine jar
> this forest is named Melagrana
>
>   O lynx, keep the edge on my cider
>   Keep it clear without cloud
>
> [p. 491:523]

Into this particular garden of the mind are allowed very obscure deities (Manitou of the Algonquins, Khardas of ?) with minor duties: keeping watch over the wine, whiskey, and cider for the bacchanal. One needs to keep in mind this buoyant flippancy when one meets religious phrases like "Kyrie eleison" midway in the lyric, or the language of devotion in its culmination:

> This Goddess was born of sea-foam
> She is lighter than air under Hesperus . . .

terrible in resistance . . .
>> a petal lighter than sea-foam
>>> aram
>>> nemus
>>> vult

O puma, sacred to Hermes, Cimbica servant of Helios.

[79/492:525]

Aphrodite was born of the sea-foam by the isle of Cythera in legend, but there is also in the phrase the Poundian undercurrent of a goddess of wind and air, a creation from nothing by the subjective poetic consciousness. To resist the impulse to poeticize the earth, make petals of foam, sacramentalize the groves, is to give oneself up to the "jungle" and "wild beasts" of reality without poetry, there where the animals are not "servants." We are, in short, here in "Melagrana" ("Pomegranate") in "that place," in the blessed lyric mood or "moment": "for three nights amid lynxes" (cf. "and for three days, and none after/Splendor" Canto 17/79:83). It is the soundless place ("Is there a sound in the forest?" p. 490:523) of the mind of Canto 17/76:80, the "dimension of stillness/and the power over wild beasts" of Cantos 47 and 49. It is the place of the "flame," the creative imagination: "This fruit has a fire within it . . . . / No glass is clearer than are the globes of this flame" (p. 490:522). The first line of the passage is reminiscent of the pregnant "bride" of Canto 39 who sings "I have eaten the flame"; the second line is reminiscent of the image of a crystal glass or sphere (pp. 457:485, 459:487) representing the spiritual wholeness when one is "within" (p. 459:488) the created moment or a created mythology. The desire is, as always, that there be many such moments: "O Lynx be many / of spotted fur and sharp ears" (p. 491:524).

For the moments are beloved whatever their status,

>> XAPITEΣ possibly in the soft air . . .
>>> in this air as of Kuanon
>> enigma forgetting the times and seasons

but this air brought her ashore a la marina
with the great shell borne on the seawaves . . .
        Eurus, Apeliota as the winds veer in periplum . . .
        as the green blade under Apeliota . . .
Time is not, Time is the evil, beloved
Beloved the hours . . .

[74/443:471]

There is terrible poignancy here summed up in the phrase "Time
is not, Time is the evil," in the "possibly," in the "enigma," and
in the "winds veer." In the moment, remembering beloved hours
and dreams, time is not; out of the moment, when the soft
winds veer to ill wind, all is doubt or enigma, darkness or
"half-light." The soft air of Kuanon/Eurus/Apeliota (the
paradisical state of mind), however, created the Aphrodite myth,
and its beauty is its own excuse for being.

        nothing matters but the quality
of the affection—
in the end—that has carved the trace in the mind
dove sta memoria

[76/457:485]

The Cavalcanti (Canto 36/178:184) is remembered together
with that ambiguous "forméd trace" in the mind that Pound
willed into being in his "translation." Here, clearly, the subjective
affection of the poet is the sculptor not a cosmic "Love" of
some absolute existence or force. All of which leads us again to
the "What thou lovest well remains" lyric of Canto 81:

        Light as the branch of Kuanon . . .
Ere the season died a-cold
Borne upon a zephyr's shoulder
I rose through the aureate sky . . .
Hast'ou fashioned so airy a mood
        To draw up leaf from the root?
Hast'ou found a cloud so light
        As seemed neither mist nor shade?. . .
        Saw but the eyes and stance between the eyes, . . .
        careless, or unaware it had not the

whole tent's room
nor was place for the full Εἰδώς . . . [Knowing]
What thou lov'st well is thy true heritage
Whose world, or mine or theirs
or is it of none?

[81/519–21:554–56]

Again the sweet breeze, the merciful goddess Kuanon, lifts the
poet to the lyric mood and mode, temporarily above nature and
time, into the limited but lovely diaphans represented by
Aphrodite's eyes. Wholly subjective? Perhaps.

and God knows what else is left of our London
my London, your London

[80/516:551]

A fat moon rises lop-sided over the mountain
The eyes, this time my world,
But pass and look *from* mine
between my lids . . .

[83/535:570]

To see the moon rise "fat," "lop-sided," is a subjective
observation out of a personal poetic vision (cf. later, "Rock's
World," p. 786:16) that is perfectly right and fitting as long as
the poet has earned his vision by close observation of the real
world first:

Ed ascoltando al leggier mormorio [and listening to the
light murmur of the breeze]
there came new subtlety of eyes into my tent
whether of spirit or hypostasis . . .
First came the seen, then thus the palpable
Elysium, though it were in the halls of hell,
What thou lovest well is thy true heritage . . .

[81/520:555]

The "seen" or "manifest" ("hypostasis"), the sea, sky, mountain,
and especially the "green" world (p. 521:556, cf. the "green
splendor," p. 432:459, the "green blade," p. 444:471) is
magnificently observed throughout *The Pisan Cantos*, no doubt

partially because of the poet's imprisoned circumstances. But the manifest offers no mystic salvation; the world is still the same dualistic heaven and hell.

> Learn of the green world what can be thy place . . .
> Thou art a beaten dog beneath the hail,
> A swollen magpie in a fitful sun,
> Half black half white
> Nor knowst'ou wing from tail . . .
>
> [81/521:556]

> man, earth: two halves of the tally . . .
> Where I lie let the thyme rise . . .
> the loneliness of death came upon me . . .
>
> [82/526:561]

The earth's heaven for man is its intrinsic beauty humanized by the poetic consciousness:

> Mist covers the breasts of Tellus-Helena . . .
>
> [77/473:503]

> Zeus lies in Ceres' bosom
>   Taishan is attended of loves . . .
>
> [81/517:552]

> clouds lift their small mountains
>   before the elder hills . . .
>
> [83/535:570]

So beautiful is the manifest that Pound cannot help feeling that there must be some design in the universe:

> nor is it for nothing that the chrysalids mate in the air
>   color di luce
>
> [74/432:459]

>   Under white clouds, cielo di Pisa
>   out of all this beauty something must come
>
> [84/539:574]

The design is apparent in the manifest, but to the Unity man's poetic spirit (Kuanon) cannot ascend.

in this air as of Kuanon . . .
By no means an orderly Dantescan rising
but as the winds veer

[74/443:471]

Merciful, however, are Kuanon's gifts, bringing us to places which the mind of man can reach: "Kuanon, the mythologies" (77/472:501). Plural, as with "Temples;" the mythologizing of life by the poetic consciousness to give life meaning, order, and ritual (religious, aesthetic, personal) is what gives the restless "hell-ridden" spirit peace. So much is clear in the following cryptic sequence of lines in *The Pisan Cantos:*

Kuanon, this stone bringeth sleep . . .
    for this stone giveth sleep
        staria senza più scosse

[74:435:462]

        [I would rest without
        further tossing, *Inferno,* XXVII:163]

"of sapphire, for this stone giveth sleep" . . .

[74/426:452]

    Her bed-posts are of sapphire
    for this stone giveth sleep.

[76/459:488]

The sapphire stone which "giveth sleep" may have neo-Platonic esoteric significance,[2] but I think the primary source is Dante in these quotations in Pound's essay on Dante in *The Spirit of Romance* (1910).

The sweet color of oriental sapphire which was gathering on the
    serene aspect of the pure air even to the first circle,
to mine eyes restored delight, as soon as I issued forth from the dead
    air, which had afflicted eyes and heart.
                    [p. 137, from *Purgatorio,* I:13–18]

Whatever melody most sweetly soundeth on earth, and doth most draw the soul unto itself, would seem a rent cloud's thundering, compared to the sound of that lyre, whereby is crowned that sapphire whereby the clearest heaven is ensapphired.

[p. 149, from *Paradiso*, XXIII: 97–102]

The sapphire in the first passage is the heavenly blue of the sky
into which Dante will ascend for as close to a beatific vision as
possible, and in the second, the sapphire is the vision in the sky
of the crowned Virgin in her blue mantle.

In the early poem "The Flame" (1911), the poet looks at
the blue of Lake Garda (Benacus) and speaks of our "immortal
moments" when "we 'pass through'" the dimensions of time
and space, through "our veils" to the "clear light," the
"thousand heavens," the domains of "many gods." "Sapphire
Benacus, in thy mists and thee / Nature herself's turned
metaphysical, / Who can look on that blue and not believe?" The
psychic moment, inspired by the blue beauty of the lake, lends
belief that fades to veils and mist once out of the moment (cf.
the "triune azures" of the same lake in "Blandula, Tenulla,
Vagula" that will inspire a "cult" of earthly delight).

In another early poem "Phanopoeia" (1918), Pound uses
some Dantesque imagery mixed with a modern ironic idiom (the
square, bedposts, and ceiling) to describe the psychic ascent (into
"light") of the poetic spirit ("flame") within its crystal sapphire
sphere:

> The swirl of light follows me through the square,
> The smoke of incense
> Mounts from the four horns of my bed-posts,
> The water-jet of gold bears us up through the
>   ceilings;
> Lapped in the gold-coloured flame I descend through
>   the aether . . .
> The swirling sphere has opened
>   and you are caught up to the skies.
> You are englobed in my sapphire.
>   Io! Io! . . .
> The folding and lapping brightness
> Has held in the air before you

You have perceived the leaves of the flame . . .
AOI!
The whirling tissue of light
    is woven and grows solid beneath us;
The sea-clear sapphire of air, the sea-dark clarity
    stretches both sea-cliffs and ocean.

The sapphire globe of light is not only above (of "air") but
beneath (of the "sea-dark clarity"), the aesthetic whole (the
sapphire globe) is of the manifest made luminous by the poet's
"flame."[3]

Implicit, too, in *The Cantos* passage's "bed-posts" are
those fashioned by Ulysses for Penelope:

                An old trunk of olive
grew like a pillar on the building plot,
and I laid out our bedroom round that tree,
lined up the stone walls, built the walls and roof,
gave it a doorway and smooth-fitting doors.
Then I lopped off the silvery leaves and branches,
hewed and shaped that stump from the roots up
into a bedpost, drilled it, let it serve
as model for the rest. I planed them all,
inlaid them all with silver, gold and ivory,
and stretched a bed between—a pliant web
of oxhide thongs dyed crimson.
       [*Odyssey*, bk 23:191–202, transl. Robert Fitzgerald]

Other literary sources may well have escaped me, and, of course,
it is highly probable that there is also personal reference to the
bed of "La Cara" (p. 459:488). But, as elsewhere in *The Cantos*,
the passages rise beyond the personal references: beautiful sea
and sky, beautiful art, beautiful lady, memories and visions, all
represented by the precious stone or crystal which "giveth sleep,"
stillness, or serenity in the midst of hellfire.

Probably also personal, yet I think universalized (albeit
cryptically), are several passages in Italian linked by an "Io son'
la Luna" motif:

E al Triedro, Cunizza
e l'altra: "Io son' la Luna." . . .

[74/438:465]

Io son la luna" . Cunizza
as the winds veer in periplum . . .

[74/443:471]

Cunizza qua al triedro,
e la scalza, . . .

from il triedro to the Castellaro . . .

la scalza: Io son' la luna
and they have broken my house

[76/452:480]

Pound, in his prison tent in view of the ruined castle on the
Pisan hill, envisions two women in the air: Cunizza who loves,
sins and is yet triumphantly placed in the Third Heaven ("terzo
cielo," Venus's) of the *Paradiso* (see bk IX, 19–66; see also
Pound's remarks on Cunizza in *The Spirit of Romance,* p. 146)
in the tent corner; and "la scalza" who is at once bereft and
triumphant. "Cunizza" may well partially represent, on the
personal level, "La Cara," and "la scalza" either an orphan waif
at Pisa or the "mia pargoletta" to whom Pound speaks later (p.
506:540). But Pound has also, by his earlier admiration for
Cunizza (see 6/22:26 and 29/14:146), by his frequent visions of
ladies in the benign air, by his recurrent images of moonlight,
half-light, of the moon nymph in *Hagoromo,* of Diana, Artemis,
and Aphrodite as moon goddesses, created a context where the
two women become variations on the visionary "Lady" that
lifts the poet from Erebus (as Beatrice and the Virgin lift Dante),
the poetic spirit temporarily lifting one from a private and a
public hell:

Cunizza's shade al triedro and that presage
in the air
which means that nothing will happen that will
be visible to the sargeants

[78/483:514]

That is, Pound's spirits rise and fall as his mind alternates between visions of heaven and hell, while the sargeants of the prison camp see nothing but the pitiful old man.[4]

Pound, in perhaps a further attempt to universalize his personal agony and triumphs at Pisa (or, as some will surely interpret it, to hide the personal), creates a variation on the "la scalza: 'Io son' la luna'" motif revolving around a pitiable little boy ("un pargoletto") rather than a little girl:

> "a S. Bartolomeo mi vidi col pargoletto,
> Chiodato a terra colle braccie aperte
> > > in forma di croce gemisti.
> > disse: Io son' la luna."
> Coi piedi sulla falce d'argento
> > mi parve di pietosa sembianza
>
> > > > > > [80/500:533]

> [at St. Bartholomeo I found myself with the little boy
> nailed to the ground with his arms spread as on the
> cross, he groaned and said "I am the moon." With his
> feet on the silvery scythe he looked pitiful to me]

Pound has seen himself in *The Pisan Cantos*, as undergoing a crucifixion ("This cross turns with the sun," p. 443:471); his "house" too had been broken, and he is "nailed" to the prison ground. So that as little boy or little girl or as the poet himself, these passages in Italian all speak of the poet's (and poetry's) pitiful, yet triumphant, condition, of praising "moonlight" barefoot (cf. "So-shu churned in the sea . . . using the long moon for a churn-stick" of Canto 2/9:13).

Or in one last cryptic variation in Italian:

> Sorella, mia sorella,
> > che ballava sobr' un zecchin'
>
> > > > > > [74/475:505]

> [sister, my sister,
> > who danced over a golden coin]

> (little sister who could dance on a sax-pence)
> > *sobr' un zecchin'!*
>
> > > > > > [78/477:508]

As with the "a San Bartolomeo" passage, a literary source is
suspected but is as yet elusive. But the linkage of the "sorella"
phrase with the "sorella la luna" (425:451) from St. Francis'
"Canzone del Sole" and with the "little daughter"
("pargoletta"), the "la scalza: 'Io son' la luna' " motif is clear.
As the moon nymph in her magic cloak ("hagoromo") dances
divinely, so the moonlight plays divinely over the Pisan
landscape, and so the spiritual light plays over the tranquil
mindscape that is temporarily Pound's.

The moon image is everywhere as prominent as that of the
sun in *The Pisan Cantos,* representing the "half-light," the "little
light in a great darkness" that is the poetic spirit's usual
condition. Pound in a depressed mood can be tough about
winter, death, the waning of the moon:

> Death's seeds move in the year
> > semina motuum
> > falling back into the trough of the sea
> > the moon's arse been chewed off by this time
>
> [80/500:534]

and scornful of the romantic weeping of youth over man's
mortality, "the young Dumas has tears thus far from the year's
end" (80/500:534). But then, in the intermittent exultant
mood, worshipful of the poetic spirit ("Artemis," "Diana,"
"Cythera" [Aphrodite], moon goddesses) as it expresses itself in
craft (at Ephesus), architecture (at Excideuil), poetry and
thought (at Mt. Segur), or social meditation (as of the "city of
Dioce"):

> At Ephesus she had compassion on silversmiths
> > revealing the paraclete
> standing in the cusp
> > of the moon . . .
>
> [80/500:534]

> and the wave pattern runs in the stone
> on the high parapet (Excideuil)
> Mt Segur and the city of Dioce

Que tous les mois avons nouvelle lune
  [every month we have a new moon]

[80/510:544]

Life's motion and flux is stilled only in art (wave pattern in
stone) and in the moment of dreams or vision. For Ephesus,
Excidueil, Mt. Segur, are all in ruins, and beautiful nature, the
manifest, asks no questions:

Tudor indeed is gone and every rose,
Blood-red, blanch-white that in the sunset glows . . .
Nor seeks the carmine petal to infer;
Nor is the white bud Time's inquisitor . . .

[80/516:551]

Man only questions the process. It is the man who must learn to
accept the beauty within it (not long for a transcendental heaven
outside it):

inexorable
                  this is from heaven
        the warp
        and the woof . . .

as some say: a dark forest
                  the warp and the woof
                  that is of heaven . . .

[80/494:527]

For men are of earth ("ΧΘΟΝΟΣ," pp. 465:494, 468:498)
and must return to it:

fluid ΧΘΟΝΟΣ o'erflowed me
    lay in the fluid ΧΘΟΝΟΣ; . . .
            fluid ΧΘΟΝΟΣ, strong as the undertow
    of the wave receding
but that a man should live in that further terror, and live . . .

[82/526:561]

The "further terror" is presumably the "loneliness of death" (p.
527:562) in the prison camp. The triumph over the loneliness is

in the poetic spirit's loving the earth's surface and mythologizing it, as Pound does with the baby wasp as Ulysses figure:

> The infant has descended,
>   from mud on the tent roof to Tellus,
> like to like colour he goes amid grass-blades
>   greeting them that dwell under XTHONOS . . .
>   to carry our news
>   . . . to them that dwell under the earth,
>   begotten of air, that shall sing in the bower
>   of Kore, . . .
> and have speech with Tiresias, Thebae . . .

                                                      [83/533:568]

"Begotten of air" as back in Canto 2, "And, out of nothing, a breathing . . . eye-glitter out of black air" (p. 8:12), or in *The Pisan Cantos,* Anchises laying hold of Aphrodite's "flanks of air" (p. 456:485), or as Pound says to and of himself, "hast'ou swum in a sea of air strip / through an aeon of nothingness, / when the raft broke and the waters went over me, . . ." (80/513:547). The struggle is to maintain, despite "fatigue deep as the grave" (p. 533:569), the poetic spirit in tragic circumstances, days where the real sun sears the eyes (p. 529:564), and the real evening moon brings the hoarfrost (p. 540:576), to maintain "hilaritas" (p. 528:563) and "amity with the hills" (p. 529:564), when the future ("Cassandra's eyes," pp. 475,7:505,8) is so fearsome, to maintain faith in the ideas of "light" or "paradise" or "whatever" (p. 528:563) in the mind.

Thus the alterations between despair and exultation—that is the form of *The Pisan Cantos.* One cannot, ought not, to deny the strong presence of the darkness, the skeptic and ironic in the dualistic tonality of these cantos and, as has been my theme, in all *The Cantos.* But though one cannot weigh its effects "on a scale" (p. 515:550), the indomitable will of the poet will not give in to the darkness, will assert those "timeless," temporary triumphs of light over darkness:

But on the high cliff Alcmene,
        Dryas, Hamadryas ac Heliades
        flowered branch and sleeve moving
        Dirce et Ixotta e che fu chiamata Primavera
                in the timeless air
        that they suddenly stand in my room here
        between me and the olive tree . . .

                                                    [76/452:480]

A motley group of ladies (mythological, literary, and real) in a
prison room! For serenity of spirit ("paradise," "elysium") can
come anyway, anywhere, anytime:

> as it might be L'Ile St. Louis for serenity, under Abélard's bridges
> for those trees are Elysium
>   for serenity
>   under Abélard's bridges
> for those trees are serenity

                                                    [80/512:546]

It is not the real sun whose light the poet is praising
(though the manifest is beautiful) but the light of the mind, not
a real breeze but a spiritual breeze, call it "love" or "Kuanon,"
the poetic consciousness:

> this breath wholly covers the mountains
>   it shines and divides
> it nourishes by its rectitude
> does no injury
> overstanding the earth it fills the nine fields
>   to heaven
>
> Boon companion to equity
>   it joins with the process
> lacking it, there is inanition . . .

                                                    [83/531:566]

The passage is, I think, marvelously precise in lyric terms about
the Poundian positions: equity is the beginning of social
consciousness, but without the poetic consciousness the social

consciousness stagnates into "dead forms" (cf. 25/118:123).
Yet to equity and the poetic consciousness must be added a
third active principle: "If deeds be not ensheaved and garnered
in the heart / there is inanition . . . (83/531:566). The mind
struggles within the historical process, its flux, tragedy and
beauty, for "distinctions of clarity" (84/539:575) between hells
and heavens of experience, societies, aesthetic artifacts, and
ethical ideas. Once those distinctions are made in the mind and
in the poem, it is necessary for the poet or the good man to act
to maintain values. Herewith are planted the seeds of triumph
and the seeds of tragedy.

# 6: THE CANTOS OF THE FIFTIES

S *ection: Rock Drill, 85-95 de los cantares*
was published by Vanni Scheiwiller in
Milan, Italy, in 1955, with American and English offset editions
in succeeding years. *Thrones, 96-109 de los cantares* was
published in Italy and (by offset) in America in 1959, followed
by an offset edition in England in 1960. *Drafts & Fragments of
Cantos CX-CXVII* was published by New Directions in 1968
and offset for the *Cantos 1-117*, New Directions volume of
1970. From all published accounts, the drafts and fragments
were written primarily in 1959-60 (the dates May 17 and 19,
1959, appear in Canto 113) and revised later for the 1968
volume. I find in these cantos of the fifties no falling off of
quality from the other cantos but, rather, refreshing new
technical triumphs, new experiments with language in new

99

audacious regions. In this view I go against a strong current in the critical literature. Being as ungenerous as possible, one can find in much of the "failing powers" attitude towards these late cantos pique in the reader who has to study them without benefit of an *Annotated Index,* and pique because *The Cantos* fail to conform to a given critic's structural predictions.[1] Not having any desire to seek structures more grand than variations on themes, I have been constantly exhilarated in reading the late cantos by the new variation, the new way of doing or looking, with the themes basically the same but richer. Canto 90, for instance, imagistically a collage of motifs from lyric passages throughout the earlier cantos, cannot possibly be understood in any precision unless the reader recollects and has responded to the contexts and precisions of those earlier lyric passages. The "brilliance," the "magnificence" of Canto 90 cannot be fully appreciated without that precise understanding. The impressionistic criticism that "appreciates" the extended lyrical passages of, say, Cantos 90–95 or Canto 106, is doing Pound little service, because this criticism is just as imprecise in its usual distaste for the nonlyrical passages. The "why" of a passage, lyric or nonlyric, defined with some precision, goes a long way towards making evident the quality of a passage and of the whole poem. There has been some excellent commentary on aspects of these late cantos, and I will refer the reader to these as I proceed. It will be my attempt to examine the lyric passages in these late cantos in the light of the earlier cantos, to demonstrate both their continuity imagistically and thematically with the earlier cantos and their enrichment of those.

SECTION: ROCK-DRILL 1955

There is no doubt that Canto 85 needs the milieu of the cantos preceding it as well as the kind of glossing of language and references to be found in the *Annotated Index.*[2] The reader who has acquired both sorts of knowledge will not find Canto

85 any more difficult than earlier cantos, perhaps less. It is to me an entertaining and rather yankee-wise run through a Chinese ethical, social, and political classic with author's marginalia:

> no mere epitome without organization.
> The sun under it all:
> Justice, d'urbanité, de prudence . . .
>
> the sheltered grass hopes, chueh, cohere . . .
>
> Hulled rice and silk at easter
> (with the *bachi* held under their aprons
> From Tang's time until now)
> That you lean 'gainst the tree of heaven,
> and know Ygdrasail
>
> [85/544:580]

Why is the sun not "over" it all? The initiate will know that the light of which Pound speaks is "not of the sun" but of the intelligence, the mind's drive for coherence, for "one ash tree in Ygdrasail" (p. 605:639), that is, for any one coherent culture amid many such (Ygdrasail, the "world tree" representing the unity that may underlie the plurality of cultures, *vide* the quotation from Frobenius in Eva Hesse's "Introduction" to *New Approaches to Ezra Pound*, pp. 45–46). The late cantos are filled with examples of cultural traditions of various lands and peoples (here the aforementioned Chinese tradition with silkworms, *bachi*, linked to a similar Italian Easter tradition) that give order and serenity to the mind:

> Sagetrieb
>
> as the hand grips the wheat,
> Risked the smoke to go forward
>
> aperiens tibi animum:
> [opening the mind to you]
> [85/559:595]

Thus ends Canto 85. Pound translates "Sagetrieb" (p. 597:632) as "oral tradition" (the "drive to say" is more literal) and adds later "thought built on Sagetrieb" (p. 686:716), as a tradition passes from peasant to poet. The mind is not limited but opened when it delights in various cultures worshiping their gods ("smoke") or venerating the earth (gripping the wheat), opened to the universal will to believe, to sanctify, and to love. From this drive comes the lyric impulse: "plus always Τέχνη / [craft] and from Τέχνη back to σεαυτόν" [of thyself] (85/546:582). The σεαυτόν may allude to Socrates' "Know thyself" and it clearly alludes in Pound's context to the "sinceritas" and "looking straight into the heart" of his Confucius. There can be no real art without technical skill or craft, or without precise examination and definition of the "Process" and humanity's place within it, so far as one can know it: "a gnomon, / Our science is from the watching of shadows" (85/543:579). And so is our art: the mind's light looking at shadows and at the local colors of the manifest "Vlaminck: '. . . is local,' 'Art is' . . . / Ver novum . . . / the faint green in spring time" (87/570-71:606-7). New art or lyric poetry ("ver novum"), new coherent mythologies, spring from a local ambience but also from the "general root" (p. 549:585), the "centrum circuli" (p. 570:606) of human desire, as "mythologies . . . establish clean values" (p. 570:606) for which man hungers. This is the basic Poundian pluralism (cf. "Temples, plural," p. 434:461, and Canto 97 passim) that is the ordering principle beneath the seeming heterogeneity of materials of these late cantos:

> Kuanon, the mythologies... (77/472:501)
>   Kuanon . . .
> and in the air αἰσσουσιν [the flames gleam]
> Bernice, late for a constellation, mythopoeia persisting,
>   (now called folc-loristica)
> reserpine clearing fungus . . .
>
>   [97/675:706]

"Mythopoeia," myth making, is the creating of gods and goddesses to explain the cosmos ("to make cosmos," p. 795:25), to order one's universe, and, more modestly, to "establish clean

values," "clear fungus." Canto 97 from pages 675–83:706–13 is
a lyric essay in comparative mythology of which some
explication will be made later. Suffice it to say here that the
focus there, as always in Pound, is on the rituals, the beautiful
effects—aesthetic, ethic, and social—of a mythology, not on its
dogmatics:

> Σελλοί sleep there on the ground
> And old Jarge held there was a tradition,
>   that was not mere epistemology.
> Mohamedans will remain,—naturally—unconverted
> If you remove houris from Paradise
>
> [87/573:609]

The Selloi's worship of Jove at Dodona (*vide* Frazer's *Golden
Bough*) was not based on rationality or philosophic logic, and
old Jarge (Santayana) understands the irrational human desire
that cannot accept another's paradise without one's customary
dancing girls, or whatever. Man's hunger for gods and paradises,
and for such ones as fit the color of his mind in his locale, is
what is natural to his nature. It is the "Natural Law" or
"Process" expressing itself in the human seed, as that seed
unfolds its "Gestalt" (p. 635:668) or inner potential for its
final form or "signature":

> In nature are signatures
>   needing no verbal tradition,
>   oak leaf never plane leaf.
>
> [87/573:609]

Man's artifacts, however, often do not come from a straight look
into the heart, from "sinceritas," and we get "false fronts,
barocco" (p. 573:609). Even with those that do, with the best
or chief, where the "altar" or "sacred grove" is achieved, the
marble or the wood block well-cut, there is always and
inevitably change and loss: "Seepage / the élan, the block, /
dissolution" (87/576:612).

The function of Canto 90 is to describe in lyric terms the

élan that is the creative moment or process; the functions of
Cantos 91–95 to dramatize again, as always in *The Cantos,* both
the achievements and their dissolution—the dualistic experience
of the human spirit in history.

> Castalia is the name of that fount in the hill's fold,
> > the sea below,
> > > narrow beach.
> Templum aedificans, not yet marble
> > "Amphion!" . . .

[90/605:639]

> Castalia like the moonlight
> > and the waves rise and fall . . .
> > to parched grass, now is rain . . .

[p. 606:640]

> . . . the light perpendicular, upward
> and to Castalia,
> > water jets from the rock
> and in the flat pool . . .
> > and the waters clear with the flowing
> Out of heaviness where no mind moves at all
> > "birds for the mind" . . .

[p. 607:641]

> > and where was nothing
> now is furry assemblage
> > and in boughs now are voices

[p. 608:642]

Castalia, daughter of Acheloüs, river god, was pursued by Apollo
until she threw herself into a fountain on Mt. Parnassus. The
spring was henceforth sacred to Apollo and the Muses. As the
motifs concerning "Castalia" in Canto 90 are brought together,
its function as a late image for the poetic consciousness is clear.
The canto is of the mind's light lifting the mind from heaviness
to Castalia, to "moonlight" or "sunlight," as singing birds rise,
lifting the poetic spirit to achievement, to light/temple/altar/
poem/building (as Amphion the walls of Thebes by his music).
Then it is that water fills the pool, spiritual rain comes to waste

land, "parched grass" turns to green "sward" again: "First petals
and then cool rain / sward Castalia again (93/624:657). Petals
before rain is backwards in nature but not in the mind: first an
image of beauty, then relief. The "furry assemblage" out of
nothing takes us back to Canto 2 and to the "ac ferae
familiares" iteration throughout *The Cantos* and throughout
this canto. We can see this in several other motifs, as the
"voices in the boughs" of Canto 3 (p. 11:15), the "birds . . .
in the branches" of Canto 17 (p. 76:80), the "larks rising at
Allegre" (Montallegre near Rapallo) of Canto 80/501:534,
Canto 107/760:785, and Canto 117/802:32. The image of birds
("grey wing, black wing," 90/608:642), here the American blue
jay, rising to represent the flight of the mind out of its personal
hell ("erebus," p. 606,8:640,2) to a personal paradise
("splendor") is given this late mythological variation (alluding
presumably to the sacred doves, Zeus's messengers, at Dodona):

> To Zeus with the six seraphs before him
>
> [90/607:641]

> Blue jay, my blue jay
> that she should take wing in the night
>
> [94/633:666]

> before Zeus, six blue jays before him
>
> [104/741:767]

> In splendour of blue-jays
>   Cythera PAGGKALA [all-beautiful]
>
> [104/744:769]

Whether to Zeus, Kuthera (Cythera), Kuanon, Sibylla, Isis,
as in this canto, or to Apollo, Thammuz, Reina, Athena, Diana,
Luna, and others later, the prayers are really always to the
godlike within us:

> quam in nobis similitudine divinae
>   reperetur imago
>
> [90/606:640]

[which in us will be found an
image of the divine likeness—Richard St. Victor]
Est deus in nobis
[It is god in us—Ovid]

[98/685:715]

which releases us temporarily from the harshness of reality:

from under the rubble heap
                    m'elevasti
from the dulled edge beyond pain
                    m'elevasti
out of Erebus, the deep-lying
    from the wind under the earth,
                    m'elevasti
from the dulled air and the dust,
                    m'elevasti
    by the great flight,
            m'elevasti

[90/606:640]

It is the poetic spirit within us that sets lights out on the water
despite the "sea's claw" (p. 607:641, cf. p. 238:249, and
p. 612:646), that builds altars in groves (cf. "aram nemus vult,"
p. 492:525), that carves altar stones under elms (p. 607:641, cf.
p. 781:11), that creates lyric visions of "phantom" trees, forests
of the imagination (p. 787:14: cf. pp. 76:80, 146:151, and
530:565):

        the trees rise
    and there is a wide sward between them .
οἱ χθόνιοι myrrh and olibanum on the altar stone
giving perfume . . .
comes flute tone
                οἱ χθόνιοι [those under the earth]
to new forest,
        thick smoke, purple, rising
bright flame now on the altar
            the crystal funnel of air
out of Erebus, the delivered,

> Tyro, Alcmene, free now, ascending
e i cavalieri,
> > ascending,
no shades more . . .

[90/608:642]

The new forest, new spring, we have seen before representing
the indomitable will of the poetic consciousness, whether
religious or lyric ("flute tone," cf. 25/119:124), to make
"crystal" from air and water (cf. p. 716:744, p. 762:786). Tyro
and Alcmene are there in Erebus, as in Odysseus's hell in Canto
1, the cavalieri were locked in the rock that the poet entered in
Canto 20 (p. 95:99). It is the poetic imagination that brings the
past (the "shades") back to life, such life as lives in art: "Trees
die & the dream remains" (90/609:643). That is, no specific
dream (one ash tree in Ygdrasail) remains, only the impulse in
men towards order and beauty: "Beatific spirits welding
together / as in one ash-tree in Ygdrasail" (90/605:639). The
choice of the curious "welding" is certainly deliberate. Heated
metals, not spirits, weld; the act of poetic will involved in
Pound's lyric moments is implicit in the "welding."

And it is implicit in his creation of the goddess "Ra-Set" in
her barge:

> Moon's barge over milk-blue water

[90/605:639]

Ra-Set over crystal . . . moving

[91/612:646]

> in the barge of Ra-Set
On river of crystal

[91/613:697]

Ra-Set in her barge now
> > over deep sapphire

[92/618:651]

The authoritative statement on "Ra-Set" is that of Boris de
Rachewiltz:

> The association of Ra and Set that we have already noted in
> the "Princess Ra-Set" may have its source in the commentary
> to the *Papiro Magico Vaticano*. . . . In this papyrus, Set, the
> god of Evil, is redeemed and allowed to enter the boat of the
> Sun-god, Ra . . . Ra-Set is therefore seen to emerge as a
> syncretic deity of the poet's invention, representing the
> essential cosmic equilibrium of good and evil (*New Approaches
> to Ezra Pound*, p. 180).[3]

That is, dualism, conquered momentarily in art in the image of
good (heaven) and evil (hell) as queen, goddess, or lady, floating
(cf. Canto 20, pp. 92–93; 96–97) in "moonlight" or on a river of
"sapphire" crystal. Castalia is the name of that river,
representing the poetic spirit's crystal achievements, made
despite the poet's swift raft journey down the quite different
Heraclitean river of change and dissolution. Canto 90, which has
described the process of poetic creation, begins and ends with a
meditation (taken from Richard St. Victor, but, as with
Cavalcanti, ultimately Pound's) on the former, not the latter,
river.

> Not love but that love flows from it
> ex animo
> & cannot ergo delight in itself
> but only in the love flowing from it.
> UBI AMOR IBI OCULUS EST.
>
> [90/609:643]

The effects of the poetic spirit or soul, of Castalia, river of the
creative imagination, express "love," but Love, the Force that
drives the will to creation, to compassion, amity, justice, is of
the Nous, ineffable.[4] Thus one finds "Where love is, there the
eye is," or said in another way, "What thou lovest well remains,
the rest is dross" (81/520:556). These maxims may seem
backwards to the rational mind, as may seem the maxim with
which Canto 90 begins, "From the colour the nature / & by the
nature the sign!" (90/605:639). "Sign" is a signature . . . "oak

leaf never plane leaf" (87/573:609). The argument (which runs
throughout *The Cantos,* especially in *Thrones*) is for the
haecceitas (thisness) of an object (i.e., its "color," cf. "a white
dog is not a dog like a black dog," p. 189:197) as more
important than its *quidditas* ("whatness") or categorization.
George Dekker is, I think, most precise on this passage:

> Color is the active mode of being of an object just as love
> is the active mode of being of the soul; and it is by the color or
> the love that we know and value an object or the soul—that is,
> by its manifestations (*The Cantos of Ezra Pound,* p. 75).

The manifest reality closely observed will register on one's
subjective feelings: "First came the seen, then thus the palpable /
Elysium" (81/521:556), . . . "that his feelings have the color of
nature" (98/689:719). But one's "world" (81/521:556), one's
"valley" (98/689:719), or "palpable Elysium," Pound keeps
saying over and over, is subjective, forms out of air, furry
assemblage out of nothing. Hence Canto 90, hence *The Cantos.*[5]

Canto 91 continues, as a major organizing motif, the image
of a flowing river or ocean wave of crystal:

> from the green deep
>   he saw it,
> in the green deep of an eye:
>   Crystal waves weaving together toward the gt/healing
> Light *compenetrans* of the spirits
> The Princess Ra-Set has climbed
>   to the great knees of stone,
> She enters protection,
>   the great cloud is about her,
> She has entered the protection of crystal . . .
> Light & the flowing crystal
>   never gin in cut glass had such clarity
> That Drake saw the splendour and wreckage
>   in that clarity
> Gods moving in crystal
>
>   [91/611:645]

Sir Francis Drake, as one more Ulysses figure, looks at the deep green of the ocean and sees, subjectively, his world of dream-vision, his lyrical order, of a Tudor civilization (one "High City" among others) impelled by the eyes of his Aphrodite, the Tudor Queen. The vision is of both splendor and wreckage. Both are part of that clarity of crystal vision, as both are part of the process ("rain also is . . . "). The "great healing" is the vision or the myth or the art work ("the production *IS* the beloved," p. 742:768). "Splendour and wreckage" is what "Princess Ra-Set" is all about. In the leitmotif of the spiritual adventurer climbing a mountain to a sacred temple, "Ra-Set" enters into crystal protection, a protection real waves do not give. Within the crystal, representing a subjective world of the poetic consciousness, gods are manifest, whatever their ontological status outside. With typical flippancy (see chap. 39 of *Guide to Kulchur,* for example,) so as to dramatize his tough stance towards "metaphysics," Pound compares crystal vision to the clarity of gin in cut glass. The "great healing" is likewise "great cloud" (clarity within, cloudy without), that is, an order of inner completeness and limpidity circumscribed by the diaphans, veils, clouds that represent the ineffability of the Nous. Thus the phrases here "great healing," "great cloud," "great crystal," and later "great acorn" (p. 755:779), "great algae" (p. 762:786), "great ball of crystal" (p. 795:25), are fraught with the poignant irony of their limitations. The fragility, the transience of crystal vision and yet its durability ("the dream remains") are stressed everywhere:

> a great river, the ghosts dipping in crystal
>
> [92/619:652]
>
>   "Ghosts dip in the crystal,
>   adorned"
> . . . A lost kind of experience?
>   scarcely,

O Queen Cytherea,
> che 'l terzo ciel movete
> [who give motion to the third heaven]
>> [91/617:650]

Ghosts of, say, Alcmene and Tyro, or of *i cavalieri,* of, that is, whatever beauty lives again in the mind of the sensitive artist or adventurer of the spirit, enter his lyric or visionary moments of splendor. Dante's "third heaven" is Venus Aphrodite's (*Paradiso,* VIII:37), with the Tenth Heaven, the Empyrean, inaccessible. "Crystal," in Pound's Dantesque framework, seems to represent the ascent of the poetic spirit from hell or Erebus through fires of purgatory ("Circe") to the light of the lower heavens:

> & from fire to crystal
>> via the body of light
>>> [91/615:649]

> that the body of light come forth
>> from the body of fire
> And that your eyes come to the surface
>> from the deep wherein they were sunken,
> Reina—for 300 years,
>> and now sunken
> That your eyes come forth from their caves
>> & light then . . .
>>> . . . by Circeo
> and the stone eyes again looking seaward
>> Thus Apollonius . . .
>>> [91/610:644]

"Reina," for the purpose of the Francis Drake motif, represents the Tudor Queen, but, far wider, she represents the "Regina Immaculata," the queen or lady conceived "out of nothing," "out of air" by the poetic consciousness. The 300 years represents the time since Elizabeth's death, also the time during which the lyrical imagination has suffered in the West, and also, simply, the very long time historically between great lyric achievements, e.g., the 180 years between Chaucer and Shakespeare noted in Canto 81/520:555. The "cave" image, representing "that place," the serenity of the poetic consciousness in its moments of splendor, is recurrent in *The Cantos*. Likewise the "Circeo" and the "stone eyes" at Terracina (pp. 195:203, 435:462, 754:779). Apollonius and the other historical and legendary figures of Canto 91 are among those people of poetic spirit who have made "crystal" from "brown leaf and twig" (p. 611:644), who come in their time to "that place": "Here Apollonius, Heydon / hither Ocellus / 'to this khan' " (91/611:645). For "hither" see Canto 17/79:83 or Canto 106/752:777; it refers as does the "khan," the "cave" and "crystal," to the mind's place, whence comes Borso and Sigismundo in Canto 17, and Drake, Apollonius, Heydon and, later in Canto 91, Layamon's Brut.[6]

Apollonius was a first-century "philosopher-in-periplum" whom Pound admired for various reasons implicit in the cryptic condensation from Philostratus's *Apollonius of Tyana* (Loeb Classics, ed., Conybeare) that occupies a large part of Canto 94 (especially pp. 636–41:669–74). In an essay in his book *Gnomon*, to which I refer the reader, Hugh Kenner has studied the Greek texts and Pound's Apollonius. I would stress only that Apollonius, like Heydon and Layamon's Brut, had a vision which illumined his life:

> We then hear in Apollonius' own words how the great
> shade appeared to him, and faded away:
>   "It was not by ditch-digging and sheep's guts . . .
>   "in Aeolis close to Methymna:
>   in the summer lightning, close upon cock-crow."
> Whereupon, to unite this interview with his
> Paradiso rather than with Odysseus' Underworld,
> Pound interpolates:

> So that walking here under the larches of Paradise
> the stream was exceedingly clear
> & almost level its margin   [*Gnomon,* p. 294]

Pound adds to Philostratus's text an image of the paradisical
state of mind (and thus creates another mask of himself). The
image had remained in Pound's mind from his early poem
(1912), "The Alchemist": "As you move among the bright
trees / As your voices, under the larches of Paradise / Make a
clear sound." The poet's chant in "The Alchemist" is to various
"ladies" of lyric song. John Heydon had a vision of a lady with
green eyes who promised him holy wisdom (Pound's
half-mocking, half-admiring attitude towards Heydon is clear in
a long passage in the original "Canto One" in *Poetry Magazine,*
August 1917; Pound is rather more respectful in his collage of
quotes from Heydon in Canto 91, p. 616:650). The central
motifs that Pound uses from Layamon's *Brut* (mentioned too in
Poetry's "Canto I") in Canto 91 (pp. 612–13:646–47) are
visions of ladies, of Brut's prayer to and vision of Diana, and the
vision that comes to the "mother of Merlin" of a "spirit bright
in cloth of gold." The Heydon motif in Pound is analyzed by
Walter Baumann in *New Approaches to Ezra Pound,* and the
Layamon motif is analyzed by Christine Brooke-Rose in the same
volume. Heydon, for all of his "half-cracked" ideas, has in his
Holy Guide some marvelous images that show that he sometimes
"dipped into crystal,"[7] images which inspired, among others, as
Baumann demonstrates, these lines in Pound:

> to ascend those high places . . .
> stirring and changeable
>   "light fighting for speed"
> and if honour and pleasure will not be ruled
>   yet the mind come to that High City . . .
> And there be who say there is no road to felicity
>   tho' swallows eat celandine
>   "before my eyes into the aether of Nature" . . .
>   [91/616:650]

so will the weasel eat rue,
and the swallows nip celandine

[92/618:651]

Pound is equally moved by Brut's prayer, "Help me to neode"
("Help me in my need," repeated in Canto 106/754-55:779)
and the later prayer of one to be laid "where lie my kindred"
(91/613:647). Pound adds to the prayer "Over harm/over hate/
overflooding, light over light," personalizing his conflation of
the medieval texts, as he has done with the Apollonius and the
Heydon texts, as he has done throughout *The Cantos* with his
conflations of myth and history. He has taken them to his
subjective self and his personal situation while, at the same
time, he has elicited from seemingly unpromising texts that
which is poetically durable, pristine images of the human
condition. Pound, in the fifties in St. Elizabeths Hospital, is in
need of help, and the prayer that he "lie by his kindred"
suggests both the personal hell he is in and the hope that his
visions, the paradises which he has set down with the help of his
Sibylle, his poetic consciousness, will place him in the book of
enduring poets.

Likewise personal, yet universal, is the Leucothea motif
that runs throughout Cantos 91, 93, 95, 96, 98, 100, 102, and
109 (and analyzed by Hugh Kenner in "Leucothea's Bikini" in
Ezra Pound: Perspectives, ed., Stock 1965, and Christine
Brooke-Rose in her *A ZBC of Ezra Pound,* 1971, pp. 138-56).
Leucothea (Cadmus's daughter, she, like a "sea gull") saves
Odysseus (see *Odyssey,* Loeb ed., bk. V:313 ff.) from drowning
in the ocean when his "raft" (see Canto 20/92-94:96-97)
overturns by giving him her magical *Kredemnon,* "veil," "scarf,"
or "bikini." As with the *molu* of Canto 47/237:247, the veil
represents for Pound the magical "diaphans" of the poetic
consciousness. The linkage of Leucothea's gift with the mind's
strength is clear:

> They who are skilled in fire
> > shall read . . . the dawn.
> Waiving no jot of the arcanum
> > (having his own mind to stand by him)
> As the sea-gull . . . said to Odysseus
> KADMOU THUGATER [Cadmus' daughter]
>
> > > > > > > > [91/615:649]
>
> > . . . bringing light *per diafana*
> "My bikini is worth yr/raft" . . .
>
> > > > > > > > [95/644,5:676,7]
>
> That the wave crashed, whirling the raft, then
> Tearing the oar from his hand,
> > > > broke mast and yard-arm
> And he was drawn down under wave,
> > The wind tossing,
> Notus, Boreas,
> > > as it were thistle-down.
> Then Leucothea had pity
>
> > > > > > > > [95/647:680]

The motif takes on further richness in *Thrones*. What is clear
from these contexts in *Rock-Drill* is Pound's relating of his own
distress to Odysseus's and to all spiritual adventurers and artists
("those who are skilled in fire") who, in exile, have only their
own minds to stand by them.

Canto 92 begins by fusing the motif of Mt. Parnassus,
whence comes the stream Castalia, with motifs from John
Heydon:

> And from this Mount were blown
> > > > seed
> and that every plant hath its seed
> > so will the weasel eat rue,
> > and the swallows nip celandine
>
> > > > > > > > [92/618:651]

In every seed is implicit its potential form, its gestalt, and, as
Heydon muses in his *Holy Guide* (and Agassiz after him), there

must be Thought in the universe if "The Weasel, when she is to
encounter the Serpent, arms herself with eating of Rue . . .
The Swallows make use of Celandine" (quoted from Baumann,
New Approaches, p. 312). Pound muses later "there is something
intelligent in the cherry-stone" (113/788:18). So, too, in man's
higher nature are the seeds of poetry, of light, of understanding,
and of love. How far the seed develops is a function of how
aware and how perceptive the poet is. The ascent of the mind
into a greater awareness of the process, and the mind's making
of beautiful things in the ascent, is allegorized in these late
cantos by a variety of motifs, dominant among them is Dante's
imagery of spheres of ascent in the *Paradiso,* but including, as
usual with Pound, many other paradigms from literary sources,
and from occult, folk, or religious sources, in none of which
Pound need have any literal belief:

> and as engraven on gold, to be unity
> but duality, brass
>   and trine to mercurial
> shall a tetrad be silver
>   with the smoke of nutmeg and frankincense
> and from this a sea-change? . . .
> & from pool of the silver circlet
>   is calm as the sapphire . . .
> To another the rain fell as of silver
>   La Luna Regina
> Not gold as in Ecbatan . . .
> Then knelt with the sphere of crystal
> That she should touch with her hands
>   Coeli Regina,
> The four altars at the four coigns of that place

                                              [92/618:651]

Heydon's *Holy Guide* is Pound's source for some of the imagery
in these lines; one does not need Heydon's alchemy, however, to
understand Pound's context.[8] We have ritual (smoke of nutmeg
and frankincense), ritual that transforms and then perishes (both
implicit in "sea-change"), ritual involved with a hierarchy of

metals: duality/brass, triune/mercury, tetrad/silver, and, finally, unity/gold (cf. the "triune azures" of "Blandula, Tenulla, Vagula," "mirrors unstill of the eternal change," and the "topaz I manage, and three sorts of blue" of Canto 5, also "The fourth; the dimension of stillness" of Canto 49). Duality is the unsatisfactory real world of experience, as always in Pound, trinity, the shifting diaphans or images of the poetic imagination, tetrad, the lyric or ecstatic or serene moment of splendor outside of time, the dimension of stillness. Thus it is that Pound can accept, in his terms, Heydon's "whole creation concerned with 'Four' " (as in the four gates of Wagadu, the four towers, Four Tuan, see Baumann, *New Approaches,* p. 315), not as a mystic about number but as a poet intrigued by the recurring imagery of four to express the human desire for catholicity, for universal knowledge from the "four corners" of the world ("and all gates are holy," p. 634:667). With "silver" is associated the "sapphire," the "crystal," and the "Luna Regina," all representative in *The Cantos* of the quietude of spirit in supreme art, serenity that the poet can attain only momentarily. With "mercury," the fluid, shifting metal, is associated the "manifest," "hypostasis" and the lesser earthly achievements that earn men places ("thrones") in the lower heavens of Dante's hierarchy (see Canto 36/179:185 and the *Paradiso,* IX:60–69). In Pound's world man usually has to settle for the lower heavens, for some poeticization of the manifest, for some justice, amity, and equity, for the ever-shifting realm of "belascio or topaz," and it is the function of *Rock-Drill* and *Thrones* in part to clearly distinguish what sorts of men are fit for which thrones.

Or in another alternate figuration of ascending spheres

> Avicenna and Algazel
> The 8th being natural science, 9th moral
> 8th the concrete, 9th the agenda,
> Agassiz with the fixed stars, Kung to the crystaline
>
> [93/625:658]

Agassiz is concerned with the natural sciences, the concrete, the manifest, the fixed stars, Kung (Confucius) with moral agenda one sphere higher, the crystalline (cf. Dante's ninth sphere, the "Primum Mobile," with the eighth, that of the "Stellar Heavens"). Agassiz searches for Thought, Intelligence in the universe by close observation of the manifest (as Pound is always demanding), Kung produces the fruit of such examination of the process: right action ("agenda", things to be done, rather than simply believed).

Or in another figuration: "Above prana, the light, / past light, the crystal. / Above crystal, the jade!" (94/634:667). "Prana" (gr.) means slope, representing presumably the hill one must climb ("where a man might carry his oar up," 23/108:112) to get above the dualism of experience to serenity of mind. Out of the light of the mind is fashioned the crystal orders of myth or society or art. Beyond is the sphere of the "jade," presumably of the inaccessible Nous, outside of time and space, of the Divine Mind.

> Le Paradis n'est pas artificiel
> > but is jagged,
> For a flash,
> > for an hour
> Then agony,
> > then an hour,
> > > then agony,
> Hilary stumbles, but the Divine Mind is abundant
> > unceasing
> > *improvisatore*
> Omniformis
> > unstill

> [92/620:653]

As St. Hilary stumbles looking at oak leaf (p. 647:679) so will Agassiz, so will Pound, in the search for Intelligence in the universe, for the nature of experience is tragically dualistic, the purpose of human agony (and much else in the Divine Mind) is

inscrutable, despite the transcendentalists who want to
"unscrew the inscrutable" (p. 724:751), to "burst out of the
universe" (p. 731:756). Thus, in this darkness and in this light,

> . . . in the great love, bewildered
>> farfalla in tempesta [butterfly in storm]
> under rain in the dark:
>>> many wings fragile
>
>   [92/619:652]

the poet, as fragile butterfly in a storm, prays in his poignant
situation to goddesses and ladies in which he can have no literal
belief,

> To Queen Nephertari this incense
>> To Isis this incense
>
>   [93/625:658]

> Lux in diafana,
>> Creatrix,
>>> oro.
> Ursula benedetta,
>> oro
> By the hours of passion,
>>> per dilettevole ore,
>>> guide your successor,
> Ysolt, Ydone,
>> have compassion,
> Picarda,
>> compassion
>
>   [93/628:661]

much as Pound did in "The Alchemist" back in 1912. For they
are all really prayers to the creative spirit within, to "Flora
Castalia," which dreams beautiful dreams despite inevitable
"storm-awakenings":

> not yet! not yet!
>> Do not awaken.
> Came then Flora Castalia

   "Air hath no petals now,
  Where shall come leaf on bough
   naught is but air.
    "pone metum, Cerinthe,
Nec deus laedit
and the Lorraine girl heard in the fields . . .

          [93/630:663]

     Such light is in sea-caves
e le bella Ciprigna
  where copper throws back the flame
from pinned eyes, the flames rise to fade
    in green air.

          [93/630:663]

The "pone metum" reference is to the lyric of Sulpicia of Canto 25/117:122, who had at least one day of splendor ("Hic mihi dies sanctus," p. 118:123), as Joan of Lorraine had her beatific moments. Then it is that "pinned eyes" open to "petaled" air, when the flame of the mind ("such light is in sea-caves") creates visions of green eyes and copper ornaments (see Canto 1/5:9) of the beautiful Cyprian Aphrodite, which then "fade in green air."

  Sulpicia's vision and Joan's vision, what status do they have ontologically? Can they burst one out of the cosmos? In Pound's view they cannot; they are as fragile as butterflies, precious petals of flowers plucked from Castalia's banks out of imperishable need and desire:

Shall two know the same in their knowing?
  You who dare Persephone's threshold,
  Beloved, do not fall apart in my hands . . .
  to enter the presence at sunrise
  up out of hell, from the labyrinth
   the path wide as a hair . . .
  You are tender as a marshmallow, my Love,
  I cannot use you as a fulcrum,
   You have stirred my mind out of dust.

Flora Castalia, your petals drift thru the air,
the wind is ½ lighted with pollen
                    diafana

                                        [93/631:664]

The beloved is subjective, diaphanous, but the drive towards
love is implicit in the human seed. The argument of *Rock Drill*
is that man by nature is "good natured" (Khati of Egypt), a
"campagnevole animale" (Dante), "naturally friendly" (Pound).
Amor lies beyond civic order, causes no blood to be shed at its
altars, "goes," but endures "5,000 years," causes paradises to be
built in the mind based on the deep-rooted feeling that "there is
something decent in the universe" (p. 647:679). The stream of
Castalia, of the creative imagination, is subsumed in the stream
of Love, poets are but a part of the great human amity. Here we
see the late humility often commented on in Pound, a humility
that would not be so surprising to some if the dualistic (rather
than mystic or arrogant) tone of the lyricism in the earlier
cantos had been more firmly grasped.

THRONES 1959

  Section: Rock-Drill ended with Leucothea saving Odysseus
from drowning by granting him her *kredemnon*. *Thrones* begins
with reference to Leucothea and her *kredemnon*, and to *muan
bpo*, which makes its first appearance:

  Κρήδεμνον . . .
  κρήδεμνον . . .
  and the wave concealed her,
                dark mass of great water . . .
  & on the hearth burned cedar and juniper . . .
          that should bear him thru these diafana

                                        [96/651:683]

And thus is ushered in the basic unifying principle of *Thrones:*

meditation on comparative mythology, which means, for Pound, comparative religion, ritual, art, language, ethics, and economics, for they are to him all intertwined. One looks for lights, for "flames in the rubble" (p. 655:687), in the darkness of history, which has always "heaped fads on Eleusis" (p. 655:687). Between Kung and Eleusis (p. 258:268), the Confucian and the Mediterranean sanity, lies the true norm of the human spirit for Pound. In Pound's view, Eleusis, broadly representing the finest moments in Western poetic consciousness (without dogmatics), does some things for the human spirit that the finest poetic consciousness of the East (without dogmatics) does not:

> This Tzu could guide you in some things,
>   but not hither,
> How to govern is from the time of Kuan Chung
>   but the cup of white gold at Patera
> Helen's breasts gave that.
>
>   [106/752:777]

"Hither" is, as always in *The Cantos,* to the mind's place: "A match flares in the eyes' hearth, / then darkness" (106/752:777). This is from the great lyric Canto 106 that illuminates the attitudes of *Thrones,* as Cantos 2, 17, 47, 81, and 90 illuminated the cantos that precede and follow them. Pound, in *Thrones,* pores over texts, ancient and obscure, as well as others not so ancient or obscure, seeking vitality of vision, poetic or social consciousness, forgotten, buried—the periwinkle eyes of the lady, representing the fortuitous lyric state of mind, shining through the rubble of history:

> aerumnae non defuerunt varia [troubles were not lacking]
>   plenty of shindies, assorted,
> With eyes pervanche, [periwinkle]
>   all under the moon is under Fortuna
>
>   [96/656:687]

The vision of history is that of the Chinese cantos. Fortuna: or in the terms of *muan bpo,* "fate's tray" (p. 785:15), compounded mostly of troubles, but also of some visions of beauty represented by "eyes pervanche." Apollonius was one of those with a vision of beauty, he was of the Eleusian spirit, and his philosophy was heaped over by the rubble and fads of history. Pound is moved, too, by the fact that the story in the *Odyssey* of Leucothea, (V:313 ff.) the water goddess who saved Ulysses off the coast of Phaeacia, has its historical continuity in the worship of a sea goddess in the form of a sea gull by the Phaeacian people:

> After 500 years, still sacrificed to that sea gull,
> a colony of Phaeacians
>
> > [96/654:686]
>
> Leucothea gave her veil to Odysseus
> Χρόνος   [Time]
> πνεῦμα θεῶν   [The soul of god]
> χαὶ ἔρως σοφίας   [and the wisdom of eros] . . .
> there is no sight without fire.
> > Thinning their oar-blades . . .
> > nothing there but an awareness . . .
> Est deus in nobis   and
> > They still offer sacrifice to that sea-gull
> est deus in nobis . . .
> > Χρήδεμνον
> She being of Cadmus line,
> > the snow's lace is spread there like sea foam
> > > [98/684-5:714-5]
>
> And after 500 years
> > still offered that shrub to the sea-gull,
> Phaeacians,
> > she being of Cadmus line
> The snow's lace washed here as sea-foam
> > > [102/728:754]

"God in us" is the poetic awareness, the fire within, that can see snow as lace. Such poetic consciousness is the saving "veil," "soul of the gods," "wisdom of love," that makes the ocean manageable. Our weapon against the sea is but the "oar," the mind's strength by which we propel our own raft by our own power.[9]

Pound is also impressed by the ancient *muan bpo* rites of the Na Khi tribe that embodied the love of one's local ambience and one's extended family, the sanctifying of these:

Without muan bpo . . . but I anticipate
      There is no substitute for a lifetime . . .
         ten thousand years heart's-tone-think-say . . .
. . . Ten thousand years say men have clans and descendents.

                              [98/691:720]

(junipers, south side) . . .
           spruce and fir take the North . . .
larix, corayana and berberis,
        after 2 stages A-tun-tzu
         a distance of one hundred *li*
Pinus armandi . . .   [101/723:750]
           under Kuanon's eye there is oak-wood. Sengper ga-mu,
To him we burn pine with white smoke,
         morning and evening.
         The hills here are blue-green with juniper,
the stream, as Achilöos there below us,
         here one man can hold the whole pass
over this mountain, at Mont Ségur the chief's cell
you can enter it sideways only . . .
With the sun and moon on her shoulders,
        the star-discs sewn on her coat
        at Li Chiang, the snow range,
                a wide meadow
and the [2]dto-'mba's face (exorcist's)
               muy simpático
by the waters of Stone Drum, . . .
Mint grows at the foot of the Snow Range . . .
                           [101/725:752]

         south slope for juniper,
Wild goose follows the sun-bird . . .
        the pine needles glow as red wire . . .
                           [102/730:756]

> Na Khi talk made out of wind noise,
>   And North Khi, not to be heard amid sounds of the forest
> but to fit in with them unperceived by the game . . .
>
> [104/738:764]

One needs to have immersed himself, as Pound did, in Joseph
Rock's very detailed, scholarly, and devoted study of the *muan
bpo* rituals ("The Muan Bpö Ceremony," *Monumenta Serica,*
vol. XIII, 1948) in order to scan all the references to the rituals
in these quotations and in others I may have missed in *Thrones,*
and then the many others in the *Drafts and Fragments* volume.
The full, scholarly handling of the *muan bpo* motif in the late
cantos would encompass Rock's earlier book, *The Ancient Na
Khi Kingdom* (Cambridge: Harvard-Yenching Institute
monographs, vols. 8-9, 1947), and his other studies of the Na
Khi, Peter Goullart's *Forgotten Kingdom* (London: John
Murray, 1955), and Pound's annotations of his copies of all of
these.[10] On first reading the *muan bpo* chants, especially in
Pound's renderings, the reverence for the things of the earth, for
local objects, the powerful symbolizing religious imagination,
the delicate poeticization of life through language and ritual, are
all clear. Clear also in Pound's collage of phrases from the chants
and their intermingling with the Latin of Rock's notes, the
interspersed Spanish, and the references to Achilous (river god)
of Greek myth and to Mt. Segur ("sacred to Helios") in
Provence, is that the drive in Pound is not to literal belief in
muan bpo, but to a pluralistic love of beautiful rites that
poeticize the earth and heavens, as in the Phaeacians worshipping
by the sea. The Phaeacians have their clans and dependents and
their rites, bound up with their *façon de voir* ("heart's
tone-think-say") and the Na Khi have theirs; without such a
poeticizing of reality of one's place by one's heart feelings, there
is no life:

> When [2]Zhi-[3]ssaw [3]ch'ung is chanted, a little wine
> is sprinkled with a juniper twig towards the altar.

While doing so the ²dto-¹mba calls the names of the
gods and spirits . . .
     Now follows the chanting of ²Zhi-³ssaw ³ch'ung . . .
     If ²Muan ¹bpö is not performed, all that which we
accomplished is not real; if ²Muan ¹bpö is not performed
we will not attain perfection like others.
(Joseph Rock, "The Muan Bpö Ceremony," *Monumenta
Serica*, vol. XIII, 1948, pp. 40–41)

Or as Pound fashions it:

> and there is
>   no glow such as of pine-needles burning
> Without ²muan   ¹bpo
>   no reality
> Wind over snow-slope agitante
>   nos otros
>   calescimus [stirring, we become
>   inflamed]
> Against jade
>   calescimus,
>   and the jade weathers dust-swirl.
>   [104/739:765]

Without such glow, such flame in the mind, the winds of reality
would not stir us to an order, a crystal. The crystal of, say,
muan bpo, while not "jade," i.e., perishable, still weathers dust
swirl for a while, especially if it finds a poet like Pound.

Pound resurrects in Cantos 96 and 97 texts such as Deacon
Paul's in Migne's *Patrologie,* various books of Alexander Del Mar
and Nicole's edition of the Byzantine *Eparch's Book,* "And the
Eparch's book was down somewhere under all of this,
ΕΠΑΡΧΙΚΟΝ ΒΙΒΛΙΟΝ" (96/654:686), seeking, especially in this
last text, precision of observation and "refinement" of language
(p. 659:691), which, for Pound, means also a refinement of
sensibility. With craft guilds, as in Byzantium, later in England
(p. 670:701), or at any time when a high standard of integrity is
demanded, as in the Eparch's edicts, precision and order is
maintained. When such standards are lost, language fails, and

ultimately the society, "with inane loquacity hoisting the wages"
(96/662:693). Thus it is that Pound, as lover of language and as
social philosopher, delights in the linguistic detail of the
Eparch's book and in debate over detail with editor Nicole. One
such moment in linguistic play of the mind instigates a cryptic
meditation (97/675–83:705–13) on language, imagery, and
perception, which leads into a subsequent meditation on
mythology and religion:

> οἶνος αἰθίοψ the gloss, probably,
> not the colour...
> as the lacquer in sunlight ἀλιπόρφυρος [deep-sea purple]
> & shall we say: russet-gold.
> > That this colour exists in the air
> not flame, not carmine, orixalxo, les xaladines
> lit by the torch-flare,
> > & from the nature the sign . . .
> > > > [97/675:706]

repeated later with variations as:

> copper and wine like a bear cub's
> > in sunlight...
> the colour as *aithiops*
> > the gloss probably
> > > *oinops*
> as lacquer in sunlight
> > haliporphuros
> > > russet-gold
> in the air, extant, not carmine, not flame, oriXalko,
> > le xaladines
> lit by the torch-flare,
> > and from the nature, the sign.
> > > > [102/730:755]

There is perhaps a play on "gloss" as linguistic definition and as
sheen of sunlight reflected from wine or lacquer. Aithiops is
"sun-burnt, dark," oinops is "wine-dark." Reflected light
registers varying colors to the eye of the perceiver and varying
associations to his subjective mind. Lacquer in sunlight and a

bear cub's skin in sunlight, for instance, have colors which the poet may associate with wine or copper color, with deep-sea purple or russet-gold. The actual colors of things in or out of sunlight are one thing; the colors with which the imagination ("flame") invests the object are another.

The rest of the detail in the passage is equally cryptic and allusive. In Canto 1, Pound refers to the second Homeric hymn to Aphrodite where the Greek poet saw Aphrodite in a crown of copper ("oricalchi") and gold. Pound is saying that one depends on such analogies to metals to express poetic or psychic vision. "le(s) xaladines" comes presumably from the Greek meaning "precious stone resembling a hailstone" (See Liddell and Scott, "xalada"), brought into French in Stuart Merrill's poem "Ballet" (1888), and quoted by Pound in his *Make It New* (Faber, p. 232). The reference in Merrill's poem is to "yeux pâles de xaladines," constituting another subjective image of a lady's eyes, here as crystal gems. Canto 90 begins with the iterated phrase, "From the colour the nature/and by the nature the sign" (p. 605:639). Its import is clear: the manifest must be observed in all its particularity to know it. But also clear in the total context is that the poet's flame, that is, his subjective mind and heart, colors the manifest (the lacquer, the bearskin).

All the detail of the passage revolves around the one idea: The "splendor 'mondan'" ("splendor of the earth," p. 676:706), the manifest, is one thing; the "pale sea-green" eyes the poet "saw once" (p. 676:707) is another. Blessed and pleasurable ("beat' è, e gode," p. 678:709) is the manifest, the "ever-shifting" (p. 677:708) change, and so are also the ever-shifting mythologies ("plenilune/phase over phase," p. 678:709, cf. the "ply over ply" motif) of new poetry, of new peoples in their "valleys," their locales or places, their *façons de voir.*

Canto 97, pp. 679–83:709–13 offers a collage of these blessed mythologies and rituals (all having the Eleusian root and the Eleusian joy in the manifest reality), a collage that can

bewilder and frustrate the reader if he is looking for some
mystic key to unite them all: Aswins, Fou-Hi, Sargon of Agade,
Multan, Napat, Panch, Tyana, Upsala, Fricco, Priapo, Venus,
The Flamen Dialis (Priests of Jove), Pomona, The Manes Di, the
rituals at Mt. Taygeto or at Rhodes:[11]

> & Spartans in Mount Taygeto
> > sacrifice a horse to the winds, . . .
> and at Rhodos, the sun's car is thrown into the sea
> rubbing their weapons with parsley,
> > Flamen Portualis
> "inter mortua jam et verba sepulta"
> > [between the now dead and buried words]
>
> > > > > > > > [97/682:713]

Those who, like Pound, respect language because they respect
the order and beauty man has made through words are the
"Priests of the gates/ between the now dead and buried words"—
not St. Peter between the now dead to be resurrected souls, but
Pound between the dead and to be resurrected words. Or, more
pointedly: "The maker of words ascending, / whiteness of bones
beneath   (98/688:718).

In these pages of comparative religion, society, and art,
Pound has made places of honor (thrones) for people like
Antoninus who "got down the percentage," for Athelstan who
"set up guilds," and for Cuillo D'Alcamo, the twelfth-century
Sicilian poet who sang "Rosa Fresca aulentissima/ c'apar' inver
la state" ("Thou sweetly-smelling fresh red rose/ that near thy
summer art"—Rosetti translation, mentioned in *The Spirit of
Romance*, p. 101). For the "Temple" of which Pound is
speaking (pp. 676–84:707–14, 721:749) is not one to any
metaphysical dogma but to the love of a good earth, good
society, good art, wherever one finds it ("and that all gates are
holy," p. 716:744):

> Earth and water dye the wind in your valley . . .
> . . . feelings have the colour of nature
>
> > > > > > > > [98/689:719]

> manners are from earth and from water
> They arise out of hills and streams
> The spirit of air is of the country
>> Men's manners cannot be one
>>> (same, identical) . . .
> Hills and streams colour the air,
>> vigour, tranquility, not one set of rules.
> Vigour, quietude, are of place . . .

[99/698-99:727-29]

That is, "art is local," love is of place, also manners, religion, and rites:

> Different each, different customs
>> but one root in the equities . . .
>> with the sun . . .
>>> under it all
>> & faith with the word

[99/699:729]

> the root veneration (from Mohamed no popery)
> to discriminate things . . .

[99/694:724]

To take away the houris from Mohammedanism and substitute dogma is to take away one of Islam's signatures, that which makes it unique, of a place and a people. The mind's light is the foundation ("under it all") for an understanding of the equities that should bind all men (the "Koine Ennoia," the "common thought," p. 695:724), and also of the manners, rituals, arts, that should discriminate finely between them and their valleys.

Selected and conflated fragments from the eighteenth-century *Sacred Edict* (a Confucian document written, as the *Eparch's Book* is written, in the koine of the people, ed., Baller, 1907) dominate Cantos 98 and 99, as examples of one magnificent social and ethical culture, one valley among all the others.

Ancestral spring making breed, a pattern . . .
& with Chou rite at the root of it
The root is thru all of it . . .

[99/707-8:736-37]

One village in order,
                one valley will reach the four seas

[p. 709:738]

                . . . village usage
                to see what style for the casting
Filiality and fraternity are the root,
Talents to be considered as branches.
Precise terminology is the first implement,
                dish and container

[pp. 710-11:739]

That the Confucian vision is different from, say, the Na Khi
vision, or the Phaeacian, or the Byzantine is not important, for
they all, at their best, have completeness, focus, harmony, roots,
and branches, are rooted in the equities, and flower with their
own signatures of art, culture, philosophy and ritual.

Unitas Charitatis,
                consuetudo diversa
[The unity of charity, the diversity of customs]

[105/749:773]

                Time mother of Manors
Nor can the King create a new custom

[109/772:796]

This last is from Canto 109 concerning Edmund Coke and
England and its great Magna Charta, which is based on English
custom and precedent. Laws, like literature, all would-be
achievements of the mind, ought to be based on precise language
and on *techne:*

                Si nomina nescis perit rerum cognitio
                        nemo artifex nascitur
[If you do not know names, the knowledge of things
will perish. No master of art is born.]

[109/772:796]

or earlier: "KAI ALOGA, / nature APHANASTON [without words, nature is not clear]" (102/730:756). Precise definition, however, does not imply abstraction, "and the sheep on Rham plains have different names / according to colour, / nouns, not one noun plus an adjective (105/747:772), but rather a sharp eye for the signatures of a given society, that which gives it unique form and "flavor" (p. 748:772), its "phylotaxis" ("oak leaf never plane leaf," pp. 743:768, 763:787, 774:798).[12] It is a lack of such awareness, such perception, that is the signature for Pound of dogmatism, fanaticism, and the hunger for transcendence: "Their mania is a lusting for farness / Blind to the olive leaf, / not seeing the oak's veins" (107/762–63:787). They are those who "want to burst out of the cosmos" (pp. 731:756, 750:775), who want "2 incarnations in every home" (p. 702:731).

The lines above are the epistemological foundations of *The Cantos* that we have stressed again and again. Cantos 100–105 attempt to lay bare this foundation with "fragments" ("mosaic? . . . You cannot leave these things out," p. 750:774), elliptical allusions to the clarity of vision of figures we have had before, Dante, Apollonius, Erigena, and others that we have not, Ambrose, Anselm, Lord Herbert of Cherbury, Remusat, Agassiz, Coke, their visions seen as a river of light descending on gemmed stones (p. 716:743), crystals, "plura diaphana" (p. 722:749). These men are poets, whether they were scientists, jurists, or philosophers, for they had the inner impulses towards order:

> Nel mezzo . . . the crystal,
> > a green yellow flash after sunset . . .
>
> > > > > > > > [100/718:745]
>
> > This aura will have, with red flash,
> > the form of a diamond . . .
>
> > > > > > > > [101/726:752]
>
> the corridor ½ an inch wide . . .
>
> > > > > > > > [105/746:771]

> ne divisibilis intellectu
> not to be split by syllogization
> to the blessed isles . . .
>
> [105/748:772]

"Isles" not "isle" as "Temples, plural" (p. 434:461) and
"nouns, not one noun" (p. 747:772). The mind makes of air
colored in one's valley (aura) "crystal" or "blessed isles," makes,
that is, a paradiso terrestre within the mind, out of its own light
(the flash "after sunset").

Which brings us to the lyrical Canto 106, wherein the poet
is again dramatizing the moment of splendour. The opening
image is of Demeter, Persephone's mother and goddess of the
underworld, and of the "Phlegethon" out of which the poet's
spirits rise.

> And was her daughter like that;
> Black as Demeter's gown,
>
> eyes, hair?
> Dis' bride, queen over Phlegethon,
> girls faint as mist about her? . . .
> A match flares in the eyes' hearth,
> then darkness
> "Venice shawls from Demeter's gown"
>
> [106/752:777]

This last is a recurring motif, representing a lingering folk
(Sabine) custom:

> no more black shawls in the Piazza
> *more Sabello,* for Demeter
>
> [98/684:714]
>
> Black shawls still worn for Demeter
> in Venice,
> in my time,
> my young time
> [102/728:754]

That the custom lingers is as moving to Pound as the fact that
the Phaeacians were still sacrificing to the sea gull after

five-hundred years (and, in fact, the two examples are put in juxtaposition on pages 684:714 and 728:754).

The image of "Apeliota" recurs in Canto 106 representing, as earlier in *The Cantos,* the intellectual breeze which inspires the mind, or, in alternate figurations, the light or flame which illumines the manifest and transfigures it:

> Apeliota
> for the gold light of wheat surging upward . . .
> granite next sea wave
> is for clarity
> deep waters reflecting all fire
> neuva lumbre, [new light]
> Earth, Air, Sea
> in the flame's barge
> [106/753:777]

Here are fused earlier motifs of the sailors of the spirit coming "hither" (p. 752:777) to "that place" with that of Ra-Set's barge moving 'neath luna. The "granite next sea wave" represents, as earlier, the clarity concerning the manifest demanded of the "sharp song" that must assimilate the destructiveness of the cliff and wave in the song's dramatization of the dualism in the process. The sea is destructive, the sacred glen creative:

> so different is sea from glen that
> the juniper is her holy bush
> between the two pine trees, not Circe . . .
> nor could enter her eyes by probing
> the light blazed behind her
> nor was this from sunset.
> Athene Pronoia,
> in hypostasis
> [106/753:778]

The juniper is from *muan bpo* but the prayer is to Athene (not Circe), her eyes seen in "hypostasis," not in a mystical state, (see 81/520:555). The mixture of East and West does not matter, for the allegory is of the mind, which does not gain blessed moments by "syllogization" ("probing") but from the mind's own flame ("the light now, not of the sun," p. 76:80): "The temple shook with Apollo . . . / light blazed behind her; / trees open, their minds stand before them" (106/754:779). Apollo, sun god, represents the inaccessible Nous; Athene, poet's muse, represents the mind's light opening to "new forest" (p. 608:642), new poetic perceptions of the manifest, or, to new images of the mind's delight, figured here, as earlier, by "Xoroi," dancing girls (cf. p. 100:104), or by birds on the wing (cf. p. 608:642): "By hundred blue-gray over their rock-pool, / Or the king-wings in migration / And in thy mind beauty, O Artemis" (106/754:779). "Artemis," moon goddess, is supplicated, as have been "Diana," "Selena," "Aphrodite," to help the poet "in need" (cf. p. 613:646), and her response (as at "Miwo") is the granting of moments of splendor that lead to new temples, new sculpture:

> At Miwo the moon's axe is renewed . . .
> Selena, foam on the wave-swirl
> Out of gold light flooding the peristyle
> Trees open in Paros
> White feet as Carrara's whiteness
> in Xoroi.
> God's eye art 'ou
> The columns gleam as if cloisonné,
> The sky is leaded with elm boughs.
> [106/755:780]

Thus out of need, out of Phlegethon, out of wave-swirl, is created the foam-born Aphrodite, columns (marble from Paros or Carrara) of temples and cities, leaded windows of cathedrals in the mind from the sanctifying of the elm tree (cf. p. 761:786, and p. 801:31). The mind is what is opened to the "divinity" in the elm leaf; the mind is "God's eye," as the creative imagination makes "crystal" from "acorn" (p. 755:779).

Or in a final lyric image of "Diana's mind" (as Artemis' mind, p. 754:779 and p. 778:8) in Canto 107:

```
      . . . her mind
            like the underwave . . .
                              the great algae
                  color prediletto [favored]
      the crystal body of air
                  deep green over azure
```

                                    [107/761-2:786]

The mind, the poetic consciousness, colors air and ocean to
make a "crystal body" of air (cf. "crystal funnel of air"
p. 608:642) or a "great algae" of water. Pound is highly
conscious of the touch of absurdity in both images (as with
"great acorn"); his purpose is to stress what he has been stressing
all along, the certain ironic distance that must be maintained in
one's art when the poet knows that there is no beauty without
belief and yet is without set belief.

DRAFTS AND FRAGMENTS 1968

According to an interview Pound granted to the *Paris
Review* in 1959 and according to other accounts more recently,
there is not likely to be much revision of or addition to the text
of *The Cantos* in Pound's posthumous papers.[13] There may be
some additions to the supposed "drafts" and "fragments" of
Cantos 110-17 as we have them, but their magnificent limpidity
of style and tone of finality in substance imply no necessary
revision to what we have been given. And what we now have can
be disappointing only to those who have some position of
special pleading about *The Cantos. The Cantos,* early and late,
have been variations on the light in the darkness: the light
affirmed, the darkness never denied. And as the inevitable
darkness comes on to the aging Pound, the light is still affirmed
though the darkness is felt more closely, even more personally,
than in the *Pisan Cantos*. The long meditative poem has, thus, at
least the curve, the form, the continuity of an organism in the
process, which is enough form for many:

Good-bye to the sun, Autumn is dying . . .
whom the ooze cannot blacken . . .

[96/663:694]

"Luce benigna, negli occhi tuoi
        Quel che voglio io, tu vuoi?
                Tu Vuoi."
[Charitable light, in your eyes,
        What I wish, do you wish?
                You wish.]

[97/680:711]

But to affirm the gold thread in the pattern . . .
A little light, like a rushlight
                to lead back to splendour.

[116/797:27]

Sun, moon, splendour, are, as they always were, representations
of the mind's serenity and exultation in its moments. In *Thrones,*
Pound, thinking of the condition of his soul or spirit as he grows
older, makes reference to that early poem (1911) of his,
"Blandula, Tenula, Vagula", "vagula, tenula / and with
splendours" (105/747:772). The Latin alludes to the Emperor
Hadrian's dying address to his soul ("O blithe little soul, Thou,
flitting away," Loeb translation). Pound muses also in *Thrones*
on Ovid's exile at Pontus (p. 736:762) and his own at St.
Elizabeths, and concludes that "Ovid had it much worse"
(p. 742:768). Pound, despite age and personal griefs, will not
despair:

The grass flower clings to its stalk under Zephyrus . . .
        are we to write a genealogy of the demons?

[114/793:23]

For the blue flash and the moments
                benedetta

[117/801:31]

A blown husk that is finished
        but the light sings eternal . . .
a pale flare over marshes

[115/794:24]

To find these moving statements or any of the others in these
drafts and fragments as confessions of the failure of *The Cantos*
is not to have been aware of the consciously wrought dualistic
and tragic tone throughout the poem, as I have tried to
demonstrate it, and as is so beautifully summed up in these lines:

> Thru the 12 Houses of Heaven
> > seeing the just and the unjust,
> > tasting the sweet and the sorry,
> Pater Helios turning . . .
> Here take thy mind's space
> And to this garden . . . ever seeking by petal, by leaf-vein
> > out of dark, and toward half-light . . .
> > > and to know beauty and death and despair
> and to think that what has been shall be,
> > flowing, ever unstill
>
> > > > > [113/786-7:16-17]

The lines echo with lines from the earlier Pound; the "half-light"
the "mind's space," the "garden," and the "petal" are recurrent
in *The Cantos;* the "unstillness" of the waves is in Canto 2 and
elsewhere; the leaf-veins, the phylotaxis, in *Rock-Drill* and
Thrones. Canto 110 picks up in its lyricism a motif with which
Canto 106 had finished:

> And in thy mind beauty, O Artemis,
> > as of mountain lakes in the dawn,
> Foam and silk are thy fingers,
> > Kuanon,
> and the long suavity of her moving . . .
> > topaz against pallor . . .
>
> > > > > [110/778:8]

The poetic consciousness ("Kuanon") makes Aphrodite of foam,
"sheathes" (silken) of air, "suavity" of ocean unstillness, and
discriminates between lovely "sorts of blue" ("topaz I manage,
and three sorts of blue," 5/17:21):

Over water bluer than midnight . . .
Here are earth's breasts mirrored
             and all Euridices,
Laurel bark sheathing the fugitive,
        a day's wraith unrooted?

                                    [110/779:9]

It is in the mind that Euridices are created, a "wraith," a
"sheath," a "diaphan," their creations a testament to. man's
deep-rooted desire for and will to Beauty. Thus, after a haunting
description of Pound's "garden" in Italy (after he was free at
last from St. Elizabeth's), the meaning of the question: "can you
see with eyes of coral or turquoise / or walk with the oak's root?"
(110/777:7). The poet's eye can love the manifest and the
process, and then "make gods out of beauty" (p. 786:16, cf. the
"vines burst from my fingers," p. 76:80), "apples from
Hesperides . . . / from phantom trees" (p. 787:17, cf. the
"floating trees" motif, pp. 76:80, 531:566, 608:642). And as
the phantoms come in lyric history, so they go:

    Soul melts into air,
                  anima into aura

                                  [111/783:13]

    And in thy mind beauty, O Artemis . . .
        Out of dark, thou, Father Helios, leadest,
    but the mind as Ixion, unstill, ever turning.

                                  [113/790:20]

There is darkness, unless beauty is resurrected by a poet like
Pound, who faces death in the spirit of a poet like Propertius:
"When the Syrian onyx is broken" (113/790:20). The allusion
is to the *Homage* (VI) where Propertius asserts that at his
enbalming there will be no fanfare, but that his "three books"
will be a "not unworthy gift to Persephone."
    Pound's "book" is of the "Verkehr," the "caracole"

(p. 777:7), turning, unstillness, that is the "Process" of nature and of the mind, and also of the stillness of the mind's moments and the serenity of orders and rites. Of the latter the *Drafts and Fragments* are full, using primarily the example of *muan bpo* and its rituals:

The nine fates and the seven . . .

[110/777:7]

heaven   earth
in the center
is
juniper
The purifications
are snow, rain, artemisia,
also dew, oak and the juniper

[110/778:8]

. . . owl, and wagtail
and huo^3-hu^2, the fire-fox
Amṛta, that is nectar . . .
If we did not perform ^{2}Ndaw ^{1}bpo
nothing is solid
without ^{2}Mua̱n ^{1}bpo
no reality . . .
Artemisia
Arundinaria
Winnowed in fate's tray
neath
luna

[112/784-5:14-5]^{14}

"From her breath"—Kuanon's breath—"were the goddesses" (p. 784:14); Pound thanks "Kuanon" for the "kindness, infinite, of her hands" (p. 788:18, 793:23). Many springs flow, many temples are built from the sanctification of the local mountain, be it "Taishan-Chocorua" (p. 530:565) or the mountain sacred to the Na Khi, Li Chiang:

By the pomegranate water,
in the clear air
over Li Chiang

The firm voice amid pine wood,
>   many springs are at the foot of
>   Hsiang Shan
By the temple pool, Lung Wang's
>   the clear discourse
>   as Jade stream

[112/784:14]

It is one world of beauty, crystal clear, not jade but "as Jade,"
this *muan bpo* world, a world forgotten until Professor Rock
resurrected it for us: "And over Li Chiang, the snow range is
turquoise / Rock's world that he saved us for memory / a thin
trace in high air" (113/786:16). Pound's question in the great
lyric of Canto 81—"Whose world, or mine or theirs/ or is it of
none?" (p. 521:556)—is not answered, nor can it be. Each
subjective world of Beauty made of the manifest can only be
entered and appreciated: "I have brought the great ball of
crystal; / who can lift it? / Can you enter the great acorn of
light?" (116/795:25).

The lyric beauties of *The Cantos* and the beauties of ritual
both aspire to a cosmic coherence or unity, but none can grasp
the inaccessible Nous, the great light of which any poet's light
("acorn of light") is but a "fragment" (pp. 781:11, 789:19), a
possible glimpse: "The marble form in the pine wood, / The
shrine seen and not seen" (110/781:11), which must remind us
of Canto 2:

Who will say in what year,
>   fleeing what band of tritons,
The smooth brows, seen, and half seen,
>   now ivory stillness.

[2/9:13]

And of Canto 81: "First came the seen, then thus the palpable /
Elysium, though it were in the halls of hell, / What thou lovest
well is thy true heritage" (81/521:556). And further Canto 90:

Grove hath its altar
>   under elms, in that temple, in silence . . .

                    the stone under elm
            Taking form now
                                                    [90/607:641]

Whether the shrine be in pine wood (cf. "under the cedars,"
3/11:15) or grove, or sacred hill, East or West, "a church/ or an
altar to Zagreus" (117/801:31), or a statue to Aphrodite, it does
not matter, for the form is one seen in the mind, formed into
images, loved, and then gone: "The Gods have not returned.
'They have never left us.' / They have not returned" (113/787:17),
which, written late, is strongly reminiscent of the early Pound:

            And shall I . . .
                confuse the thing I see
        With actual gods behind me?
                Are they gods behind me?
                        ["Canto I," *Poetry,* June 1917, p. 121]

Whether one's vision is of an absolute truth or not cannot be
known. Man's mind is a "hall of mirrors" (p. 793:23), a
"labyrinth" (p. 799:29), his art a "dance in a maze" (p. 793:23),
the paradise he is given is to "see, not walk on" (p. 796:26),
that is, he is given perceptions of beauty and not, so far as he
knows, any immortality beyond his "painted paradises." The
poet is blessed in these moments that are as a "gold mermaid up
from black water" (p. 783:13); he creates the emerald crystal
that is condemned eventually to "seeping" (p. 789:19, cf.
p. 576:612). He is like a butterfly in a storm ("farfalla in
tempesta," p. 619:652). But so important is its gift to man that
poetic consciousness is at the same time divine guide: "Two
mice and a moth my guides— / To have heard the farfalla
gasping / as toward a bridge over worlds . . ." (117/802:32).
    Psyche, the soul, took the form of a butterfly in the myth
(see Apuleius), and the poet's soul has the power within that
can carry him temporarily "out of erebus" into the blessed
"paradise terrestre" of the mind, to "that place" that the lyric
mode of Pound's *Cantos* has always represented.

 NOTES

CHAPTER ONE

    1. The critical and metacritical debate concerning Pound's theology or philosophy runs the gamut from Pound as shallow atheist to confirmed mystic, neo-Platonic, or other. To experience the full dimensions of the disagreements, the reader would need to consult almost all of the citations in the Bibliography below. The reader who has not first read the poetry and prose of Ezra Pound aided only by the *Annotated Index* sort of information begins such reading at his peril. Part Two of *Ezra Pound: Selected Prose* (ed. William Cookson, New Directions, 1973), especially "Axiomata" (1921), gathers many of the relevant prose texts of Pound on his "beliefs."

    2. Pound's "aesthetics" are only slightly less furiously debated than his theology. Again, *The Cantos* is the massive effect of an aesthetic and should be the primary object of study. Pound's critical prose, for which I share Marshall McLuhan's enthusiasm, incessantly talks aesthetics. I would refer the reader to *The Spirit of Romance*, the *Literary Essays*, and the *Guide to Kulchur* as companions to *The Cantos*, and to the Gaudier-Brzeska, Arnold Dolmetsch, and Brancusi essays for Pound's sense of "imagism" as "total context," "myth" as "explications of mood," and "crystal" as "formal perfection or pattern."

143

3. *Vide,* to quote only from two of Pound's most intelligent exegetes:

It follows that such exegesis [of Canto 91] as has just been attempted
is necessarily wide of the mark and wrong-headed for, since it proceeds
by raising to the explicitness of ideas matters that the poet goes to great
lengths not to make thus explicit, the reading that exegesis offers is
necessarily a travesty of what the poetry means and is. Perhaps this is
true of all poetry whatever, but it is true to such a degree of the *Cantos*
that Pound seems to have had before him, as one main objective, the
baffling and defeating of commentators and exegetes. (Donald Davie,
Ezra Pound, p. 229)

One thing, however, is certain: my exposition of Canto 90 leaves many
of its secrets intact . . . those who wish to gain wisdom will probably
do well to look elsewhere, perhaps in the books from which Pound
mined these cantos. Even the cantos which have much or some beauty—
i.e., 90–93 and 106—are maddeningly cryptic . . . . (George Dekker,
The Cantos of Ezra Pound, pp. 83, 199)

The slight tone of pique and/or condescension in these remarks (which Pound often
invites) grows to elephantine proportions in some other criticisms. My position is
simply that more probing will untangle the cryptic and make more precise the exegesis
of the future.

4. 15:19, 109:114, 119:124, 201:209, 457:485–86, 611:645, 795:25.
5. 66–69:70–73, 77:81, 236–38:246–48.
6. 77:81, 89–90:93–94, 195:203, 238–39:248–49.
7. 109:114, 119:124, 195:203, 435:461.
8. 76:80, 146:151, 530:565–66.
9. 18:22, 78:82, 236:246, 607:641, 612:646.

CHAPTER TWO

1. Walter Baumann in his *The Rose in the Steel Dust* has a line-by-line study
of Canto 4, as does *The Analyst* for Canto 4 and for all of the first eleven cantos. I am
therefore handling these early cantos only in overview to demonstrate the tonality of
"gold in the gloom," of "little light in a great darkness," which sets the tone for the
lyrical passages throughout *The Cantos.* Guy Davenport has an extended analysis of
Canto 4 in *Wisconsin Studies in Contemporary Literature,* 3:2, and George Dekker of
Canto 7 in his *The Cantos of Ezra Pound.* Sister M. Bernetta Quinn in her "The
Metamorphoses of Ezra Pound" (*Motive and Method in The Cantos of Ezra Pound* ed.,
Leary) is one of the first scholars to explore the mythological or lyrical passages in
The Cantos, and subsequent studies are indebted to her. The student of the early
cantos will find indispensable *The Annotated Index,* and hardly less so, Clark Emery's
Ideas in Action and Hugh Kenner's *The Poetry of Ezra Pound.* Myles Slatin's "A
History of Ezra Pound's Cantos I–XVI, 1915–1925" (*American Literature,* May 1963,
pp. 183–95) is a useful summary.

2. In the *Dial* of May 1922 (pp. 505–9), there appeared "Eighth Canto"

which is not a Malatesta Canto but, in fact, what becomes Canto 2, minus its first five lines. The *Dial* version's opening lines are these:

Dido choked up with tears for dead Sichaeus;
And the weeping Muse, weeping, widowed, and willing,
The weeping Muse
                    Mourns Homer,
Mourns the days of long song,
Mourns for the breath of the singers,
Winds stretching out, seas pulling to eastward,
Heaving breath of the oarsmen,
                    triremes under Cyprus,
The long course of the seas,
The words woven in wind-wrack,
                    salt spray over voices.
Tyro to shoreward lies lithe with Neptunus
And the glass-clear wave arches over them . . .

Clear in these lines, which form a transition from Canto 7 and which are omitted in the final Canto 2, is the counterpoising of lyric song (almost buried in Pound's contemporary scene and mourned for only by the few) against "wind-wrack" and "salt spray" of time and "desensitization" (92/622:654) of the poetic consciousness (which can "see" Tyro and Neptune in waves). The importance of the theme of the poetic consciousness in *The Cantos* is demonstrated by "Eighth Canto" becoming "Canto 2."

CHAPTER THREE

1.   Perhaps the only question I have with Hugh Kenner's seminal writings on Pound is in Kenner's view of the "floating forests of marble" imagery of Canto 17 as "sinister":

In Canto XVII the vanished Greek landscape of vines, clear water, and goddesses is reproduced by the Venetians in a "forest of marble." That the Venice Cantos—like Venice itself—possess great beauty no one denies. There is a limitation inherent in **static** beauty of this sort, however. . . . As in the stone forest, art by defying living process comes close to being a perversion of nature. . . . All these attempts to educe stability from the flux, setting up a dead queen, fabricating a stone forest, are against nature, "contra naturam" (Canto XLV). They apotheosize the arrest of living processes. . . . They are part of Pound's "Inferno," not his "Paradiso." The great paradox of the poem, and one of its structural keys, is, then, that the conventionally splendid passages in the first third of the work deal with dead material. (*Motive and Method in The Cantos of Ezra Pound,* pp. 20-22)

My reading of these motifs is that the paradisical state of mind is dramatized by Pound in his lyrical passages as well through images from art and architecture as from nature and from mythology, i.e., that there is no implication of perversion intended in the "stone forest" image (cf. Bibliography: Quinn, pp. 88–89; Emery, p. 31; Davie, pp. 122–29; Brooke-Rose [in *Ezra Pound: Perspectives*], p. 156). Kenner's position concerning the Venice motif ("most complexly ambiguous") in his *The Pound Era* (1971, pp. 342–48; 419–23) is perhaps a shade different tonally.

2. Professor Kenner, in kind answer to my inquiry, sees the concluding passage of Canto 20 as a "baroque equivalent" to the "revelation of Aphrodite" structural motif throughout *The Cantos;* the connotations are of "blatancy," "Vanoka" as a "false Aphrodite," the description leading up to her appearance resembling "a heavy allegorical painting." Eva Hesse, in her bilingual edition of Cantos I–XXX (Verlag der Arche, 1964, p. 326), relates "Vanoka" to the historical Vanozza Catanei, mistress of Pope Alexander VI and mother of Lucrecia Borgia (="Madame Hyle" of Canto 30). I would refer the reader also to Donald Davie's *Ezra Pound,* chapter VII, on Cantos 17 and 20 (wherein I agree with his remarks on the "marble trees in water" motif and disagree with those on the "not of the sun" and "lotophagoi" motifs).

3. My reading of this difficult passage is that the "clear shapes" are the "basis of renewal," not the "confusion" or "wilderness." The syntax is ambivalent. The clear shapes in the mind are the "lozenge of the pavement," which cryptic phrase I would translate as something like "the forms imagined within reality."

4. For the debate in the Pound literature concerning "forma" and "concetto," see below, Chapter Six, n. 4.

5. An excellent line-by-line analysis of Canto 23 is the essay of T. L. Tarson prepared for a seminar of N. H. Pearson at Yale, made available to me in xerox copy from the Yale University Library. Sharon M. Libera in her "Casting His Gods Back into the NOUS" (*Paideuma,* 2:3) is very precise on the neo-Platonists Iamblichus and Gemistus Plethon, who influenced Pound, but when she speaks of Pound "neo-Platonizing" his Confucian material, I would say rather that Pound Confucianized his neo-Platonism.

6. The sexual theme in *The Cantos,* especially Cantos 29, 39 and 47, is traced by George Dekker in his *The Cantos of Ezra Pound,* often, I think, to the point of making it dominant rather than subordinate to the aesthetic theme, as I have tried to present it.

CHAPTER FOUR

1. Cf. George Dekker in his *The Cantos of Ezra Pound,* chapter VI, section 3, "Canto 36 as a 'Translation.'" Dekker is quite right that the "translation" is Pound's poem, not Cavalcanti's, but I find his conclusion as to Pound's "intentions" rather dubious:

> My comparisons have one main object: to establish how Pound has quite consciously written a 'translation' which, while developing and emphasizing certain ideas quite clearly, succeeds in communicating one primary quality of the original—its impenetrability.

So as, if I follow Dekker, to keep the reader humble about the "Nous."

2. The exultant "bride" does not, I feel, contain in its multivalency an

allusion to Penelope, as Forrest Read, Jr., in *Motive and Method in The Cantos of Ezra Pound*, p. 109, and Daniel Pearlman in *The Barb of Time*, p. 163, see it, though the Ulysses motif in the canto makes the association compelling. The image is of impregnation by Zeus to create a god, not by Ulysses to create a Telemachus.

3. Donald Davie in his *Ezra Pound: Poet as Sculptor*, pp. 154-58, sees Canto 47 as equally of the aesthetic and the sexual life. George Dekker shifts Davie's emphasis toward the sexual theme in his *The Cantos of Ezra Pound*, chapter II, "Fertility Ritual in *The Cantos*," pp. 37-46, and Daniel Pearlman in his *The Barb of Time*, pp. 172-92, extends the sexual theme and fertility ritual idea into a scheme of triads of vegetation cycles and of attainment of "Cosmic Consciousness." The canto (and *The Cantos*) is, in my reading, primarily of the aesthetic experience or state of consciousness.

4. Daniel Pearlman in his *The Barb of Time*, Appendix B, pp. 304-11, "The Source of the Seven Lakes Canto" (49), publishes translations of the short poems in Chinese and Japanese from which Pound created part of the canto. But, as with the Cavalcanti of Canto 36,

> The freedom with which Pound selected images and "translated" them
> becomes immediately evident. The need to study Canto 49 as an
> integral, self-consistent, poetic structure entirely original with Pound is
> to be emphasized beyond dispute . . .

to which I can only add my agreement. Hugh Kenner, in his "More on the Seven Lakes Canto" (*Paideuma* 2:1), prints the actual translations Pound worked from to create his canto.

5. For these relationships, see Hugh Kenner's *The Pound Era*, pp. 455-56, though it seems to me that Pound was conscious of the relationships earlier than there asserted.

CHAPTER FIVE

1. Allen Neame has a helpful analysis of lines 1-42 of Canto 74 in the *European*, no. 4, and in subsequent issues of lines 207-16, 453-65, 588-98. Walter Baumann analyzes Canto 82 in detail in his *The Rose in the Steel Dust*. Daniel Pearlman has a long chapter on *The Pisan Cantos* in his *The Barb of Time*. Clark Emery's book is still perhaps the most useful source of information and insight on *The Pisan Cantos*, along with Kenner's writings passim and, of course, the *Annotated Index*.

2. Walter Baumann in *New Approaches to Ezra Pound* ed., Hesse, p. 313, notes that the sapphire and its "signature" of "giving sleep" may be mentioned in occult literature of John Heydon's sort. It does not, so far as I can see, appear in Heydon, though the Euterpe vision (Book VI) speaks of "Saphiricks of the Sun and Moon" and of bedposts of ivory. In Pound's *Letters* (p. 30), the phrase "gnostic gem" appears in a context concerning Allen Upward, which suggests further areas of search. Michael Shuldiner, in "Pound's Progress: The 'Pisan Cantos'" in *Paideuma* 4:1, cites a sapphire-bedecked bed in the medieval "Letter of Prester John" as the source for Pound's image. My initial reaction is that both probably go back to an earlier source.

3. N. Christoph DeNagy in his *The Poetry of Ezra Pound: The Pre-Imagist Stage*, 1960, analyzes "The Flame" (pp. 36-52 passim) and concludes, as I do, that the image of the flame represents poetic "inspiration" and the "sapphire Benacus" the secluded world of the poet's imagination (cf. also, Allen Upward, *The New Word*

[New York: Mitchell Kennerley, 1910], chap. 14, "Metastrophe; the Magic Crystal")
Eva Hesse, in kind response to enquiries of mine, notes these lines in "Horae Beatae
Inscriptio" (*Personae*, p. 65):

> How will these hours, when we twain are gray,
> Turned in their sapphire tide, come flooding o'er us!

where the "sapphire tide" represents, it seems, the poetization of memories.

4. Eva Hesse notes that "il Triedro" and "the Castellaro" have personal
reference for Pound in the Rapallo-St Ambroglio area.

CHAPTER SIX

1. Dekker and Davie, in particular, seem to disembark from the late cantos,
particularly *Thrones,* too early. Noel Stock, who has soured on Pound and his ideas,
is, for all his impatience, helpful in his researches into the late cantos. Daniel
Pearlman, for all his respect for the intellectual positions and formal structures in *The
Cantos,* curiously feels the poet has said it all by *The Pisan Cantos* and calls the
post-Pisan material a "denouement," despite what 250 pages of denouement says for
Pound's sense of structure in *The Cantos.*

2. There are some useful notes to Cantos 85-87 by D. D. Paige in *The Pound
Newsletter,* no. 6, on these cantos and *Rock-Drill* in general in Hugh Kenner's
Gnomon, pp. 280-96, and on *Thrones* in Kenner's *The Pound Era,* pp. 532-35. Other
books with emphases on the later cantos in the Bibliography are those by Brooke-Rose,
Davie, Hesse, and Stock. See also the magazines *Agenda* and *Paideuma.*

3. As DeRachewiltz makes clear, the deities fused in Pound's "Princess
Ra-set" were male in the ancient Egyptian books; further evidence that Pound's
lyrical visions carry no literal belief in any mythology. Pound's *Confucius* has this
from the master: "To seek mysteries in the obscure, poking into magic and
committing eccentricities in order to be talked about later; this I do not" (p. 113).
DeRachewiltz's essay "Pagan and Magic Elements in Ezra Pound's Works" is very
helpful in its bringing together of sources for Pound's late meditations in comparative
mythology, and incisive in its sense of the distance Pound keeps between himself and
these materials.

4. Ever since Pound in the *Guide to Kulchur* used the phrase "The forma, the
immortal concetto" (p. 152), there has been debate as to what the words meant to
Pound. In terms of the later "Gestalt seed" idea, we can look back at the phrase and
see the "forma" of a living thing as the full actualized potential of the seed, in other
words, its manifest "signature." In aesthetics, then, the "forma" would be the
"crystal," the full working out of the concept or "concetto," the achieved act,
harmonious in all its parts. As the "signature" is potential in the seed, so is the forma
in the concetto. The "forma" is, then, different from the Platonic "Form" in that in a
Platonic system all living things and all intellectual achievement yearn toward the
transcendental Ideal which cannot be manifest in the phenomenological world.
Donald Davie's remarks on "forma" and "crystal" (*Ezra Pound: Poet as Sculptor,*
Chapter XII, "The Rock-Drill Cantos") hover, it seems to me, between a Platonic and
a non-Platonic interpretation. Eva Hesse (in her "Introduction" to *New Approaches
to Ezra Pound*) seems to define "forma" ("early phrase of ideation," pp. 15, 48)

much as Davie defines "fantasy" (p. 218). The debate over "forma" is really but an aspect of the larger debate over Pound's theology and philosophy as outlined above in my Chapter One.

5. The subjectivity of one's sense of another person or his vision ("But Sordello, and my Sordello?" 2/6:10; "Whose world, or mine or theirs . . .?" 81/521:556; "This time my world," 83/535:570; "Rock's world," 113/786:16) is, I think, what is meant by the cryptic "and was Erigena ours?" 90/605:639, i.e., is the Erigena of *The Cantos* much like the historical Erigena, and does it matter?

6. Folquet, the Provençal poet, was another who had a "vision" of a lady (92/619:652; see Pound's *The Spirit of Romance,* p. 56), and is thus described as "nel terzo cielo" when he did so.

7. Pound's openness for all sorts of thinkers, like John Heydon, for the poetic consciousness they may exhibit, extends itself into the willingness to accept the cryptic—the "trobar clus"—in poetry. In the Cavalcanti essay in *Literary Essays,* Pound demonstrates on pp. 178-82 the cryptic language of a number of major poetic texts, and this is one of the examples: "What is the magic river 'filled full of lamias' that Guido sends to Pinella in return for her caravan?" (p. 180, the reference is to Guido's sonnet translated by Pound in his *Translations,* pp. 58-59). The Heydon passages and the Cavalcanti passage appear together in *The Cantos* in 91/616:650, with Cavalcanti's "magic river" becoming a variation on the "Castalia" motif.

8. John Heydon, *Holy Guide* (1662), book II, chapters 3-6, on the powers of the numbers 1-4, relates unity to gold, duality to brass, trinity to mercury, tetrad to silver, and on page 49 is mentioned nutmeg and frankincense as gifts to an angel who can be made to appear by talismanically engraving the number four in silver.

9. The similarity in name to Leucothea presumably causes Pound to think of the story of Leucothoe (Ovid's *Metamorphoses* IV, 194 ff.) and to use it in *The Cantos* (98/685:715, 102/728-30:754-56, studied in Brooke-Rose, pp. 150-56). She, like Castalia, resisted Apollo but finally succumbed to him. Her father had her killed and buried; she rose again by the power of Apollo's light as an incense bush. The fragrant bush, as Castalia's crystal stream, or Luecothea's diaphanous veil, represents the poetical transformation of harsh reality.

10. Two studies have recently appeared on the Na Khi motif in *The Cantos,* both in *Agenda* vol. 9, nos. 2-3: John Peck's "Landscape as Ceremony in the Later Cantos" and Jamila Ismail's "News of the Universe: Muan Bpo and The Cantos." Both offer needed scholarship into the documents of Na Khi at Pound's hand, and highly intelligent exegesis (in the case of the Peck article, over a wide range of the later cantos), though both place different emphases on the functioning of the motif in *The Cantos* than I have in my remarks. See also C. F. Terrell, "The Na-Khi Documents," *Paideuma* 3:1:91-122.

11. Details of the mythological figures in these pages, especially 97/679-80:710, may be found in Noel Stock's *Poet in Exile,* pp. 254-56, and Boris DeRachewiltz, *New Approaches to Ezra Pound,* pp. 187-88. John Peck, in an article "Pound's Lexical Mythography" in *Paideuma* 1:1, focuses on explication of two passages from Canto 97, while ranging in some highly elliptical prose over *The Cantos* in general and *Thrones* in particular. Pound's source for the evocative word "xaladines" in the Stuart Merrill poem was pointed out for me by Professor Hugh Kenner, who must spend much of his time helping students of Pound.

12. Pound, in another figuration of the "phylotaxis" or "Gestalt seed" idea, says that "form is from the lute's neck" (p. 716:744), "form is cut in the lute's neck,

tone is from the bowl" (p. 774:798). That is, one can only get such music from the lute as is inherent in its nature, its construction, its limitations; just as man can only make poetry (his "crystal" or "high city") of the process as he experiences it in his "valley," the coloration of his mind. This coloration, the subjectivity of the poet as person ("my world," Rock's, Sordello's, Browning's "world"), is the "tone" of the given poet's instrument.

13. See *The Paris Review*, no. 28, 1962, pp. 49–49; also Mary DeRachewiltz (Pound's daughter) in *Esquire* 15:4 (April 1966):179; Harry Meacham, *The Caged Panther* (New York: Twayne Publishers, 1967), p. 190; Alan Levy, *The New York Times Magazine*, Jan. 9, 1972, p. 64. The *Paris Review* interview is an important document of the late thinking of Pound. With respect to the subject and positions of this book, I would refer the reader to the full context of statements in the interview such as "The Confucian universe as I see it is a universe of interacting strains and tensions" (p. 23); "bad language is *bound* to make in addition bad government" (p. 41); "Another struggle has been the struggle to keep the value of a local and particular character, of a particular culture in this awful maelstrom, this awful avalanche toward uniformity. The whole fight is for the conservation of the individual soul. The enemy is the suppression of history; against us is the bewildering propaganda and brainwash, luxury and violence" (p. 43); "I am trying to collect the record of the top flights of the mind. I might have done better to put Agassiz on top instead of Confucius" (p. 47).

14. In the articles by Peck and Ismail cited in note 10, above, Pound's use in Canto 110 of a tragic love and suicide tale from the Na Khi literature as transcribed by Rock is clearly demonstrated as the source of phrases such as "eye of coral" and "the nine fates and the seven." Not so clear is the extent to which one ought to interpret Pound's intent from the tale's burden, as Peck and Ismail do. As with all of Pound's usage of sources, the appeal must be to the context in *The Cantos*, not to the source.

# BIBLIOGRAPHY

For all writings by Ezra Pound in chronological order, see Donald
Gallup's *A Bibliography of Ezra Pound*, Rupert Hart-Davis, London, 1969.
Indispensable for scholarly research on *The Cantos*.

ANALYST, THE, ed. Robert Mayo, Evanston: Northwestern University,
     1953–   , mimeographed sheets, line-by-line analyses of Cantos
     1–11.
ANNOTATED INDEX TO THE CANTOS OF EZRA POUND, eds., John
     Edwards and William Vasse, Berkeley and Los Angeles: University of
     California Press, 1959. Glosses Cantos 1–84. Indispensable.
BAUMANN, WALTER. *The Rose in the Steel Dust*, Coral Gables:
     University of Miami Press, 1970. Detailed analysis of Cantos 4 and
     82.
BROOKE-ROSE, CHRISTINE. *A ZBC of Ezra Pound*. London: Faber and
     Faber, 1971.

DAVIE, DONALD. *Ezra Pound: Poet as Sculptor.* New York: Oxford
University Press, 1964.

DEKKER, GEORGE. *The Cantos of Ezra Pound.* New York: Barnes and
Noble, 1963.

DENAGY, CHRISTOPH. *The Poetry of Ezra Pound: The Pre-Imagist Stage.*
Bern: Francke Verlag, 1960; idem, *Ezra Pound's Poetics and Literary
Tradition.* Bern: Francke Verlag, 1966.

EMERY, CLARK. *Ideas into Action.* Coral Gables: University of Miami
Press, 1958.

ESPEY, JOHN. *Ezra Pound's Mauberley.* Berkeley and Los Angeles:
University of California Press, 1955.

FRASER, G. S. *Ezra Pound.* New York: Grove Press, 1961.

HESSE, EVA, ed. *New Approaches to Ezra Pound.* Berkeley and Los
Angeles: University of California Press, 1969. Indispensable collection
of criticism, includes essays by Eva Hesse, Richard Ellmann, N.
Christoph DeNagy, Forrest Read, Guy Davenport, Boris deRachewiltz,
Donald Davie, J. P. Sullivan, Christine Brooke-Rose, George Dekker,
Walter Baumann, John Espey, Hugh Kenner, Albert Cook, and Leslie
Fielder.

JACKSON, THOMAS H. *The Early Poetry of Ezra Pound.* Cambridge:
Harvard University Press, 1968.

KENNER, HUGH. *The Poetry of Ezra Pound.* Norfolk: New Directions,
1951; idem, *Gnomon,* New York: McDowell Obolensky, 1958;
idem, *The Pound Era.* Berkeley and Los Angeles: University of
California Press, 1971.

LEARY, LEWIS, ed. *Motive and Method in the Cantos of Ezra Pound.*
New York: Columbia University Press, 1954; essays by Hugh Kenner,
Guy Davenport, Sister M. Bernetta Quinn, and Forrest Read, Jr.

MINER, EARL. *The Japanese Tradition in British and American Literature.*
Princeton: Princeton University Press, 1958.

PAIDEUMA, ed., Carroll Terrell, University of Maine, Orono, Maine, 1972,
devoted to Pound studies.

PEARLMAN, DANIEL. *The Barb of Time: On the Unity of Ezra Pound's
Cantos.* New York: Oxford University Press, 1969.

POUND NEWSLETTER, THE, ed. John Edwards, University of California,
Berkeley, 10 issues, 1954–56, compendium of information on Pound
and *The Cantos* collected for the *Annotated Index.*

ROSENTHAL, M. L. *A Primer of Ezra Pound.* New York: Macmillan,
1960.

RUSSELL, PETER, ed. *An Examination of Ezra Pound.* Norfolk: New
    Directions, 1950. Important early collection of essays: T. S. Eliot,
    Edith Sitwell, Allen Tate, Ernest Hemingway, George Seferis, Hugh
    Kenner, John Drummond, Charles Madge, D. S. Carne-Ross, Ronald
    Duncan, Marshall McLuhan, G. S. Fraser, Henry Swabey, Hugh
    Gordon Porteus, Max Wykes-Joyce, Brian Soper, John Heath-Stubbs,
    and Wyndham Lewis.
RUTHVEN, K. K. *A Guide to Ezra Pound's Personae (1926).* Berkeley
    and Los Angeles: University of California Press, 1969.
SCHNEIDAU, HERBERT. *Ezra Pound: The Image and the Real.* Baton
    Rouge: Louisiana State Unitersity Press, 1969, on Pound's aesthetics.
STOCK, NOEL. *Poet in Exile: Ezra Pound.* Manchester, England:
    Manchester University Press, 1964; idem, ed. *Ezra Pound:*
    Perspectives. Chicago: Henry Regnery, 1965, essays by Noel Stock,
    Conrad Aiken, Herbert Read, Marianne Moore, Hugh Kenner,
    A. Alvarez, Peter Whigham, Donald Gallup, Allen Tate, Hugh
    MacDiarmid, William Fleming, Ernest Hemingway, Christine
    Brooke-Rose, Tom Scott, Wyndham Lewis, Joseph Malof, and Denis
    Goacher; idem, *Reading the Cantos.* New York: Random House,
    1966.
SUTTON, WALTER, ed. *Ezra Pound: A Collection of Critical Essays.*
    Englewood Cliffs: Prentice-Hall, 1963, essays by Walter Sutton,
    William Butler Yeats, William Carlos Williams, T. S. Eliot, F. R.
    Leavis, Hugh Kenner, M. L. Rosenthal, Forrest Read, David Evans,
    W. M. Frohock, Harold Watts, Earl Miner, Murray Schafer, J. P.
    Sullivan, George P. Elliott, and Roy Harvey Pearce.
WATTS, HAROLD. *Ezra Pound and the Cantos.* Chicago: Henry Regnery,
    1952. On Pound's philosophy.
WITEMEYER, HUGH. *The Poetry of Ezra Pound 1908–1920.* Berkeley and
    Los Angeles: University of California Press, 1969.

INDEX

155

Library of Congress Cataloging in Publication Data

Nassar, Eugene Paul.
    The Cantos of Ezra Pound.

    Bibliography: p. 151
    Includes index.
    1. Pound, Ezra Loomis, 1885-1972. The cantos.
I. Title.
PS3531.082C2865   811'.5'2   75-11343
ISBN 0-8018-1703-X